STATE AND COSMOS
IN THE ART OF TENOCHTITLAN

RICHARD FRASER TOWNSEND

Dumbarton Oaks   Trustees for Harvard University   Washington, D.C. 1979

To my parents, with whom I first traveled
in the Valley of Mexico

ACKNOWLEDGMENTS

This study was written as a doctoral dissertation for the Department of Fine Arts at Harvard University, in 1974, and has been published here with minimal changes. I wish to express my gratitude to Miss Tatiana Proskouriakoff, whose lectures on Mesoamerican art and religion were touchstones for many of the thoughts expressed herein, and who, as my adviser, offered patient, quiet guidance. Dr. John Rosenfield similarly gave invaluable advice and criticism, as did Dr. Oleg Grabar; both these teachers opened fields of thought in the Far Eastern and Islamic traditions that I continue to draw upon for understanding Mesoamerican art and architecture. Dr. Evon Vogt's Harvard Chiapas Project Seminar also introduced me to ideas that have proven to be fundamental. My wife, Pala Townsend, read through many difficult passages in the thesis manuscript, which she helped to clarify; her faith and interest, and her curiosity as an artist, have always been a source of strength. In conclusion, I would like to thank all the numerous friends in Mexico City and Zacualpan, Morelos, in whose care I was for many months during the time of research on this project.

RFT
Austin, Texas
March, 1977

Contents

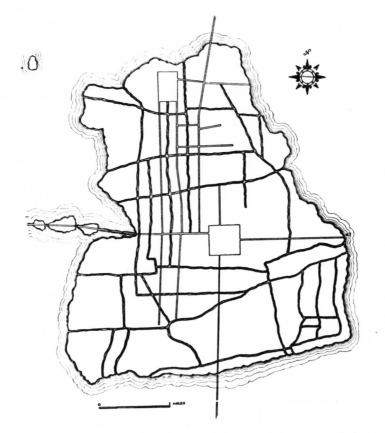

Fig. 1 Reconstructed map of the city of Tenochtitlan, showing the fourfold division and the location of the main ceremonial center. The Tlatelolco ceremonial and market center is to the north of downtown Tenochtitlan (after Sahagún 1951–70, Bk. 12: Frontispiece).

Themes of Monumental Art at Tenochtitlan

Setting: City and Landscape

On November 12, 1519, the Emperor Moctezuma Xocoyotzin took Hernan Cortés by the hand atop the Tlatelolco pyramid and invited him to admire the view of Tenochtitlan, capital city of the Mexica nation. Below them an immense crowd moved through the greatest marketplace in the land, attracted in unusual numbers by the news of the arrival of the Spanish expedition with their Tlaxcalan Indian allies only four days before. Hundreds of canoes could be seen traveling across Lake Texcoco to the canals and landing places of the island metropolis. Over a mile to the south of the Tlatelolco district lay the main ceremonial precinct of Tenochtitlan itself—a spacious, cardinally oriented quadrangle with a processional way, pyramid-temples, ritual concourses, and schools. Four principal streets led from the gates of this most sacred space of the Mexica empire, dividing the city into quarters (Fig. 1). The palaces of Moctezuma and earlier emperors lay just outside the precinct wall, forming an ensemble that expressed the proximity of government and religious institutions. Elsewhere throughout the city a multitude of lesser ward temples and the red-and-white plastered houses of the notables stood out clearly from thousands of wattle-and-daub thatch houses that filled out the residential quarters. Almost all these buildings stood upon *chinampas*, the enormously fertile garden plots of reclaimed land, constructed of layers of rich lake-bottom mud held in place by stakes, wattles, and slender willow trees that gave stability while allowing a maximum amount of sunlight to come through (Fig. 2). A regular grid of footpaths and walkways provided communication in addition to the canal system, but there were no wheeled vehicles and no beasts of burden; trade and tribute alike entered the city on the backs of long strings of human carriers, or in the bottoms of canoes. Bernal Díaz del Castillo, who accompanied the party of Cortés and Moctezuma at the Tlatelolco pyramid on that November day, further describes the panorama:

And so we were looking, for that great and accursed temple stood so high that it commanded all very well; and from it we saw the three causeways which enter into Mexico—that of Ixtapalapa, which is the one by which we had entered four days ago, that of Tacuba, which was the one where we later left fleeing on the night of our great defeat . . . , and that of Tepeyacac; and we saw the sweet water [aqueduct] which came from Chapultepec to provide the city, and upon the three causeways the bridges placed at intervals, under which the water from the lake flowed from one place to the next. . . . (Díaz del Castillo 1904, I: 290; author's translation)

The inhabitants of Tenochtitlan called themselves Mexica in the Nahuatl language, and in this passage Bernal Díaz uses the tribal term as the name of the city—Mexico. The well-known name "Aztec" was originally a generic term applied to various Nahuatl-speaking tribes who traced their origin to the quasi-mythical Aztatlan; the Mexica became popularly known as Aztecs only since the nineteenth century.

The major causeways linking Tenochtitlan and the lakeshore communities led on to roads and paths through the fertile piedmont cornfields and beyond, to the dark sierras rimming the valley. These mountains are still covered with chilly forests of oak, pine, fir, and alder, and the land is cleared and terraced around many ancient towns scattered throughout the higher elevations. To the south and southwest of the valley, the vista is contained by a majestic volcanic escarpment with cinder cones, lava flows, and the eternally snowcapped peaks of Popocatepetl and Ixtacci-

Fig. 2 Above, detail of a sixteenth-century map of Tenochtitlan (after Maudslay 1909). Note long rectangular *chinampas*, canals, footpaths, small local temples, and a larger temple of the type at Santa Cecilia Acatitlan, D.F. (right). Maguey cacti grow in front of the temple.

huatl, rising to altitudes of over 17,000 feet above sea level. The valley floor lies at an altitude of about 7,000 feet, and, before the mid-twentieth-century smog of industrial Mexico City, the air had a pure, cool transparency and a luminosity that was intensified by reflections from the now-vanished lake. March, April, and May are the dry months, when parched fields are swept by dusty winds; during the latter part of this season, people wait for rain with the same anticipation that the first warm day of spring is waited for in northern climates. The rains arrive in June and last until late fall; in this season great thunderclouds build up over the major volcanic peaks during the late morning hours, and by early afternoon a black storm begins to sweep up along the line of the southern escarpment, catching on the summits and then breaking open to engulf the entire range and adjacent portions of the valley in sheets of rain and violent electrical discharges.

Lake Texcoco was the largest body of water in a system of five interconnected lakes that made the Valley of Mexico the most ecologically diverse of all the basins in the Central Highlands (Fig. 3). This valley is separated from its neighbors by abrupt, but easily traversed mountain ranges. The neighboring basins vary in altitude from about 8,000 feet in the chilly, formerly swampy and forested Valley of Toluca to the west, to approximately 7,000 feet in the more temperate, partially irrigated Valley of Puebla to the east; to the south, the volcanic range drops off vertically in baroquely contoured cliffs to the warm, verdant Cuernavaca Valley, which at the 5,000-foot level has long been a source of tropical and semi-tropical products. The fertility of this southern region starkly contrasts with the northern end of the Valley of Mexico, which already begins to shade away into the semi-desert Chichimeca—a lonely steppe broken by intermittent tan sierras, covered with mesquite trees, thorny brush, and spiny succulents.

From their vantage-point at Tlatelolco, the Mexica emperor and his Spanish guests appreciated the view of Tenochtitlan and the surrounding countryside for many of the same reasons: it was a place of excep-

tional physical beauty, unimaginable wealth, and fearsome authority, charged with a presence of greatness that was remarked by Indians and Spanish alike. But the perceptions of the two peoples differed in certain fundamental respects. As we shall see in following chapters, the Mexica saw the relationship between their city and its natural environment as an integrated cosmological structure—an ordered universe within which the natural phenomena were regarded as intrinsically sacred, alive, and intimately relatable to the activities of man. This outlook contrasted with that of the Europeans, who saw cities as artifacts of civilization —places where religious and legal institutions sharply distinguished man's identity from that of untamed nature. The Spanish friars and soldiers automatically placed themselves as human beings on a higher level than other forms of life in a hierarchy of Creation. But the Indians approached the phenomena of nature with a sense of participation: the universe was seen as reflections of relationships between life forces, and every aspect of life was part of an interpenetrating cosmic system.

This notion of a living structural affinity between the natural and the social orders was a governing principle of Mexica religious and state ideology; monumental architecture and sculpture at Tenochtitlan was directly concerned with the representation of that idea.

Mexica History: Migrant Tribesmen and Urban Dwellers

In addition to describing the association between man and nature, the art of Tenochtitlan was concerned with the commemoration of Mexica historical identity: the origins of the nation, the processes and events that marked the rise of Tenochtitlan to a place of preeminence in Mesoamerica, and the institutions that evolved in the formation of a tributary empire. For this reason it will be useful to review a few basic facts of Mexica history as it is presently known to us.

The Central Highlands had been the setting for a metropolitan civilization for well over a thousand

Fig. 3 Map of Central Highland Mexico, showing extent of the original lake system and the location of Tenochtitlan (after Sahagún 1951–70, Bk. 12: Frontispiece).

years before Tenochtitlan was founded in 1325. Ruined cities of earlier peoples are dispersed throughout the region, attesting to an ancient heritage. The attractions of the Central Highlands—a wealth of natural resources, the splendor of the cities, a superior agricultural technology, and a more highly developed social organization—stood in contrast to the semi-desert northern Chichimeca, inhabited by simple agricul-

turists and nomadic bands of hunters and gatherers who largely lived beyond the pale of Mesoamerican civilization. Such marginal tribesmen had been filtering down to the Central Highlands since at least the seventh-century collapse of Classic Teotihuacan. The Mexica were only the most recent of these northern migrants to seek their fortunes in the urban region.

The complex interactions of migrant tribesmen with

the urban heirs of Classic culture constituted a long, continuous process of acculturation—a dominant aspect of Postclassic Mesoamerican history. Acculturation was not a simple matter of assimilation of the less sophisticated by established complex societies, nor one of onslaught and overthrow by invading barbarian hordes. It was instead a process of synthesis, compromise, and consolidation, as newcomers settled, developed individual cultural variations from pre-existing patterns, and in time asserted the new identity of their communities. The process of acculturation produced cultural transformations over a period of centuries in Postclassic times, which were marked by the rise of military aristocracies, a generally warlike tenor, and political fragmentation. However, the archaeological record shows that basic economic and technological patterns persisted; and architectural and sculptural remains reveal many formal continuities as new groups created monumental settings for themselves which were at once different from those of earlier peoples or contemporary rivals, while utilizing many of the same symbolic elements. Mexica acculturation to urban life follows this general pattern.

It appears that the wandering Mexica tribe first made contact with urban Mesoamerica at the eleventh–twelfth century Toltec city of Tula, where they were perhaps employed as military mercenaries. But after the destruction of Tula by still unknown peoples they sojourned among the petty kingdoms of the Valley of Mexico for some two centuries, earning for themselves a reputation as skilled warriors while simultaneously being despised as uncivilized barbarians.

Tenochtitlan itself was founded only after an ignominious altercation with the Lord of Culhuacan, who forced the Mexica to flee his land to the unclaimed rocky outcrops and mud flats of Lake Texcoco. During the following decades the Mexica enlarged their marshy refuge through the *chinampa* system, and established a small marketplace, which, apart from its economic importance, was indispensable for making social and political contacts. The Mexica ruler Huitzilihuitl (who reigned from about 1396 to 1416) and his counselors promoted constant trade with other nations; Mexica traders moved from one place to another, exchanging the humble resources of their island environment—fish, frogs, and vegetables.

They began to fill their city with people from neighboring towns and to take them in marriage.

In this way they won over the people of Texcoco and others. They treated travelers and strangers well, they invited merchants to come to the markets of Mexico with their goods for such commerce always enriches a city. (And this same Aztec nation today has this quality; to towns where a man is well received and flattered and given to eat and drink he will go willingly, especially if he sees inviting faces, which is what most appeals to him.) (Durán 1964: 44)

As the Mexica became consolidated as an urban people, they were inevitably drawn into the tributary system. In this system, defeated nations were required to send laborers, manufactures, and natural resources to their conquerors on a regular basis. This was an ancient, well-established aspect of economic life in Central Highland Mexico. In its early stage, Tenochtitlan paid tribute to the powerful city of Azcapotzalco, located on the nearby western lakeshore. But by the 1420s Tenochtitlan initiated a war of independence and entered into formal military alliance with the prestigious lakeshore city of Texcoco (itself the capital of a sizeable tributary domain) and the lesser city of Tlacopan. Azcapotzalco was defeated and its possessions distributed among the victors, who then exploited their successes with a series of campaigns of conquest that soon extended beyond the Central Highlands. During this time Tenochtitlan began to enter a new phase of its cultural, military, and economic life. Texcoco and Tlacopan continued to enjoy a privileged, if sometimes strained, position in the new order, but their political importance slowly declined as Tenochtitlan grew in power. So fearsome were the Mexica armies, and so dreaded the rulers of Tenochtitlan, that even the forceful king Nezahuacoyotl of Texcoco saw fit to caution the magnates of his nation:

I beg you fondly, lords and brothers, to watch how you treat the Mexicans. Flee from their enmity and from encounters with them. Let us have perpetual peace and inviolable friendship with them. You already know them; it is not befitting to declare myself in particular concerning their condition. If you meet them upon the roads and they ask for some of what you carry, share with them, caress them, for in so doing we lose nothing, and to do the contrary is to gain nothing if it be not war and troubles, death, robbery, and shedding of our blood and desolation of our province. (Martínez 1972: 233; author's translation)

By the 1470s, scarcely fifty years before Cortés was welcomed on the Ixtapalapa causeway by Moctezuma Xocoyotzin, Tenochtitlan was well on the way to becoming a metropolitan imperial capital. Mexica conquests extended down to the steamy tropical coast of Veracruz, south to the ancient Zapotec and Mixtec territories in Oaxaca, and beyond to the Pacific coast of Guatemala; by the time of the Spanish arrival, Mexica traders were operating regularly at Xicalango on the Gulf coast of Campeche—a presage of eventual military campaigns in Maya lands. To be sure, the power of Tenochtitlan was not unresisted: Mexica expeditions had not successfully penetrated the Tarascan realm of Michoacan, and even within the Central Highlands the Tlaxcalan nation fiercely maintained its independence. Nevertheless, by 1519 Tenochtitlan undisputably exerted the greatest centralizing political, economic, and cultural force in Mesoamerica.

As with many imperial nations of Europe or Asia, it became important for the Mexica to commemorate their history, not necessarily as it had actually happened, but as it was officially interpreted after the policy of systematic conquest was initiated. It is a well-known fact that early Mexica histories were destroyed and new ones commissioned by order of Itzcoatl and his famous vizier, Tlacaelel, during the 1420s. As the capital acquired an increasingly metropolitan character, it was equipped with monuments that commemorated the historical achievements of the nation according to the dictates of imperial policy and ambition. But the concerns of state and religion were inseparably associated at Tenochtitlan, and historical events were iconographically depicted in terms of ritual procedures unfolding upon stark cosmological settings. In Mexica sculptural iconography, figures and hieroglyphics blend, and the functions of art and writing were compounded in a visual code meant to be read by the inhabitants of Tenochtitlan and their visitors alike.

Themes of Monumental Art at Tenochtitlan

During the century before the arrival of Cortés, public architecture and sculpture were created at Tenochtitlan, put together from forms borrowed and assimilated from earlier sources. In effect, this new imperial tradition is the last and most visible manifestation of the acculturation process that has been recounted. Ever since the nineteenth century, scholars have described the stylistic character of Mexica art, its basic symbols and symbol clusters, and more recently, the sources the Mexica drew upon in forming their new art. Numerous studies have also been devoted to iconographic interpretation, yet at this time we have only a fragmentary picture of the conceptual world these images portray: elements of myth, of metaphysical speculation, and history have been found, but the picture of an integrated ideological structure remains elusive. It is the purpose of this study to establish the outlines of this conceptual underpinning by examining three interrelated themes of Mexica sculptural iconography: (1) the manner in which it illustrated the structure of the universe and expressed its sacred character; (2) the manner in which it represented the fusion of the social order and the national territory with this cosmological structure; and (3) the manner in which it represented Tenochtitlan as the triumphant, sovereign, and historically legitimate successor to an ancient civilization. These three themes were automatically and almost inseparably interwoven to affirm Mexica national identity in time and space, to communicate the validity of their state and to justify its policies, and to foment a sense of mission that would lend impetus to military conquest.

Problems in Decoding Mexica Art

Continuity or Disjunction?

As a newly formed imperial art, how does Mexica sculpture symbolically differ, and in what ways does it maintain continuity with the past? Do forms assimilated from the past change meaning to express unique, specifically Mexica concerns? Or is there at some level a persisting pattern of meaning that can be related to the more obscurely understood cultures of Classic and even Preclassic times? Is there in fact some larger ideological integrity to the many Mesoamerican cultures whose collective history spans at least 2,500 years, or do discontinuities evident in the archaeological record indicate fundamental ruptures and radical reorganizations in the cultural fabric? Does the art of Tenochtitlan represent a major break, or is it simply a rephrasing of traditionally held images and ideas? Any study of Mexica art must be addressed in some measure to this complex and much-debated problem (see especially Kubler 1967, 1969, 1970, 1973; Willey 1973; Coe 1973; and Nicholson 1973).

The study of Mexica art occupies a pivotal position for us in understanding Mesoamerican civilization because it is uniquely accompanied by literary documents—the pictorial screenfold "divinatory manuals" of native and early colonial manufacture, and the detailed descriptions of Indian life by friars, soldiers, and second-generation historians of mixed ethnic and cultural background. Any attempt to unravel the meaning of earlier Mesoamerican art must take into account this last and most accessible phase of the entire tradition. For this reason, it has long been standard practice to use Mexica art and its associated ethnohistoric sources for the purpose of interpreting Classic and even Preclassic iconography.

Michael Coe is perhaps the most vocal proponent today for the view that the symbolism of Classic and Preclassic iconographic systems is to be understood through study of the sixteenth-century Mexica monuments and documents. In Coe's view, almost all the Mesoamerican area can be regarded as an *oikumene* of shared belief and symbolism. Unfortunately, the vast majority of iconographic studies using Mexica monuments as keys to the past suffer in two respects: first, Mexica art itself has not been sufficiently interpreted, and, second, it cannot be assumed uncritically that configurations of form and meaning peculiar to the fifteenth century may be projected back as far as the first millennium B.C. The dangers of using the Postclassic sources in this manner have been pointed out by George Kubler, who in recent publications has called attention to the phenomenon of iconographic disjunction in the Western European tradition between the art of Late Classical Antiquity and that of the High and Later Middle Ages. It has been noted that, wherever in the High and Later Middle Ages a work of art borrowed its form from a Classical model, this form was almost invariably invested with non-Classical, normally Christian significance; on the other hand, forms that apparently were purely Medieval and Christian could also, on occasion, be invested with meanings derived from Classical learning (Panofsky 1960). Arguing against the frequent assumption that similar forms in different periods and places must invariably carry similar meaning, Kubler draws the following parallel:

Similar examples of disjunction between classic and post-classic form and meaning can be supposed in highland Mexico. . . . Such disjunctions make it improbable that Aztec texts can be used to explain classic Maya continuities of form and meaning. Continuity of form, or of meaning, cannot be assumed to prevail without disjunction where durations on the order of a thousand years or longer are involved. Thus it is misleading to suppose uncritically that classic Maya sculpture and post-classic Maya manuscripts belong to the same cultural duration. They belong to different religious frames of reference and the formal continuities between them cannot be assumed to imply continuity of meaning without further proofs. (Kubler 1969: 8)

In another recent article on the art of the Central Highlands, Kubler noted that the sixteenth-century ethnohistoric sources on the rituals of Tenochtitlan cannot be used to explain the murals of Teotihuacan, painted a thousand years earlier, for the same reason that the Hellenistic images of Palmyra should not be interpreted by using Arabic texts on Islamic ritual (Kubler 1973: 166). Consequently Kubler has abstained from using sixteenth-century sources as a key to earlier art, focusing instead on descriptions of the structure and dynamics of discrete iconographic systems as a first step in understanding their function and meaning.

Kubler's analogies with Western European, Hellenistic, and Islamic art have drawn criticism from Gordon Willey, who has pointed to three assumptions that have been traditionally held among archaeologists familiar with the specific data of Mesoamerica. The first is that Mesoamerica can be viewed as a unified cultural tradition, that the component cultures within its boundaries are more closely related to each other than any one of them was to outside cultures, which is to say that all Mesoamerican cultures were linked in time and space in a single cultural universe or civilization. The second assumption is that within this major cultural system there was a unified ideological system embracing religion and abstract intellectual thought. And the third assumption is that "there was an integrity of belief and communication within this Mesoamerican ideological system that permits us, in archaeological retrospect, to ascribe similar meanings to similar signs and symbols" (Willey 1973: 154). These three assumptions underlie the method of "direct historical approach," which is concerned with working back from the living to the dead in order to reconstruct and understand the past (see also Nicholson 1973: 72). Supporting these views with a review of the archaeological record, Willey suggested a basic Mesoamerican pattern of synthesis, dissolution, and resynthesis of a basic inventory of themes, as opposed to the compartmentalization of cultures and ideologies suggested by the analogy of disjunction.

Willey's critical remarks are not directed against the principle of disjunction as such in Mesoamerica, but rather to the use of analogy with Western Europe or the Middle East without sufficient reference to specific archaeological and ethnohistoric information available on different Mesoamerican cultures. The analogies of Late Classical Antiquity and the High and Late Middle Ages, or of Palmyra and Islamic culture, as examples of disjunction over long periods of time could easily be countered with other analogies to illustrate the possibility of continuity. For example, themes persist with changes of form, and configurations of form and meaning may indeed endure over great spans of time, as is illustrated by the history of art in India, and by the Buddhist arts of Tibet, China, Japan, and Southeast Asia. The disjunctive situations that abound in Asian history do not rule out ideological continuities. Indeed, the rich variety of Buddhist art is attributable to the generative capacity, flexibility, and adaptability of religious ideals; diverse sects reflect different methods for the attainment of their ideals, each with a distinctive iconography relating this quest to the social and physical environment of the time and place (Rosenfield and Shimada 1970). If one is looking for analogies, such a pattern would seem to fit the synthesis, dissolution, and resynthesis described by Willey. Doubtlessly, there were great differences in emphasis between Classic and Postclassic religious and political structures, but such differences do not necessarily rule out the possibility that ideas concerning the relationship between state and cosmos remained largely unchanged in Mesoamerica. In other words, there may exist a matrix of ideas to which all or many Mesoamerican iconographic systems refer, even if they interpret this matrix according to specialized, local cultural interests. Thus, by distinguishing certain underlying themes within the iconographic system of Tenochtitlan, the level at which continuity is to be found may become apparent. Analogies drawn with other art traditions are useful when taken as suggestive guidelines, subject to modification according to specific contexts. Though Kubler's analogies may be countered, his observations are valuable in calling attention to the need for rigorously critical treatment of the Late Postclassic sources and the need to understand fully the implications of the patterns of change that are apt to occur within historical processes. Only under these conditions can the transformation or the persistence of meaning be fully appreciated.

If Mexica iconography is to be made fully relevant to its own past, it must be understood in the context of an historical process—namely, the process in which this monumental ensemble was formed, and came to be so clearly distinguishable in the spectrum of Mesoamerican art. What is the magnitude of disjunction represented by this process? At what level is it possible to speak of continuity of meaning, and at what level does change occur? In a word, what is the historical phenomenon that took place at Tenochtitlan from about 1427, when the Mexica nation began its imperial expansion under king Itzcoatl, to 1519, when Cortés and his allies beheld the capital that would lie in ruins within two years time?

The Formation of Mexica Sculpture

Mexica sculpture was above all cosmopolitan, for it was composed of a variety of forms deliberately chosen from earlier and contemporary traditions. By utilizing a selected inventory of forms that expressed widely held religious and secular ideas, the Mexica formed an art that would help to integrate their realm ideologically, and that would simultaneously serve to affirm the Mexica as legitimate successors to the great nations of the past. This incorporation speaks of a Mexica ambition to assimilate an ancient hallowed heritage—a tendency towards continuity. But Mexica sculpture is not merely imitative. For all its borrowings, this art is far from being a mechanical pastiche: the innovations and stylistically integrated character of Mexica art also indicate a determination to affirm a uniquely Mexica identity. Ironically, the synthesis that they brought about seems almost to isolate the Mexica culturally—a tendency towards disjunction. The following three sources of Mexica sculpture will serve to exemplify the tension between the borrowing of older forms and their transformations in the cosmopolitan environment of Tenochtitlan. This will help us to identify the pattern of a process; the outline

of this pattern will help us to assess the level at which continuity was maintained with past tradition, and the level at which disjunction was most likely to have occurred.

The first source for Mexica sculptural imagery is found in the pictorial-screenfold ritual manuscripts of the Valley of Puebla and adjacent regions, a conservative area known as the Mixteca-Puebla that had remained less transformed by the incursions of migrant barbarian groups than the Valley of Mexico. The most ancient focus of stability in the Valley of Puebla was the religious and mercantile city of Chollolan (Cholula). As Nicholson (1971b: 396-7) has pointed out, the pictorial manuscript tradition may be in fact the most direct descendant of Classic Mesoamerican art. This tradition is the most likely vehicle for transmitting ideological principles of great antiquity. The Borgia Codex is often cited as a quintessential example of these Mixteca-Puebla polychromatic manuscripts (Fig. 4). Figures are represented in flat colors with strong linear outlines, with no attempt to create illusions of stereometric space. Settings are represented by place-glyphs, cosmological symbols for the earth or sky, or sectioned buildings. Anthropomorphic figures are depicted in stylized profile poses, but there is no concern for individual portraiture; instead, personages are identified through meticulously detailed articles of ritual attire, cult artifacts, and other accessories. However, personages are identified by name-glyphs in Mixtec dynastic histories. The formal canons of manuscript illumination also regulated the polychrome ceramics of this region, and greatly influenced wallpainting and the lapidary arts (Fig. 16). It has been traditionally held that manuscript illumination influenced relief sculpture, but it is also likely that influences flowed in reverse, in a system of mutually exchanging imagery. A glance at the Stone of Tizoc (Figs. 19, 20) or the Dedication Stone (Fig. 17)—both celebrated historical commemorative monuments that will be discussed later in detail—immediately reveals the close affinity between Mexica sculptural relief and the pictorial manuscript tradition.

The second source for Mexica sculpture was ar-

15

Fig. 4 Details from the Codex Borgia, pp. 14, 28. Right, a ritual figure approaches a temple; below, a cosmological setting.

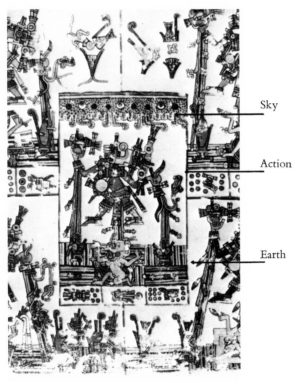

Sky

Action

Earth

chaeological. Large-scale sculpture seems to have suffered a temporary eclipse in the Central Highlands after the twelfth-century collapse of the Toltec capital of Tula, although there are some indications that the tradition persisted in vestigial form among the petty states of the Valley of Mexico prior to the rise of Tenochtitlan. Literary references mention the fact that sculptors were brought from Azcapotzalco to work at Tenochtitlan after the Tepanec defeat, but unfortunately there is little archaeology that would help to clarify the extent and style of fourteenth-century "pre-Mexica" sculpture (Nicholson 1971a: 112–3). It is usually assumed that figures of Toltec origin were directly imported from ruined sites to serve as models in the sculpture workshops of the capital. In effect, the use of sculpture in the Toltec mode represents a facet of historicism and revival. Two celebrated warrior figures illustrate this matter. One of these sculptures (Fig. 5) is stylistically so close to the famous "atlanteans" of Tula that it was long thought to have been removed from that archaeological site. Like Toltec prototypes, it has a planar format: articles of clothing and the face, hands, and feet remain close to the monolithic matrix. It is impersonal, with hardly even a suggestion of ethnic type; only the insignia and identifying garments are executed in detail. Another standing warrior figure (Fig. 6) shows how the sculptors of Tenochtitlan developed this type into more uniquely Mexica forms. This second figure is also quite symmetrical, and, while the relationship between planar elements can hardly be described as fluid, there is greater animation and variety to the relief. Details are executed with fine lines, superimposed articles of clothing are more decisively blocked out and differentiated by deep incisions, and surfaces are carefully modeled—note especially the comparatively soft and swelling quality of the face, which not only accurately represents an ethnic type, but is also charged with greater expressive power and vitality, as if a pneumatic force had begun to press the outer surfaces from within. Other figures in the round such as "standard-bearers" (seated figures holding flagpoles) and "chac-mools" (recumbent figures holding ritual receptacles upon their midriffs) were also reproduced with similar stylistic and iconographic transformations. It is reasonably certain that such figures borrowed from Toltec tradition depict guards, minor officials, and ritual functionaries of palace and temple whose presence reinforced the pomp and pageantry of public ceremonial. These figures are of an entirely different category from anthropomorphic cult effigies, which form the third major source of Mexica sculpture that will serve to illustrate the pattern of the formative process.

Anthropomorphic cult effigies proliferated in great variety at Tenochtitlan and in neighboring cities of the Central Highlands, but there is no significant precedent for them in earlier Central Highland art (Figs. 7, 8). It is highly likely that their sources lie in the Huaxteca region of northern Veracruz, eastern San Luis Potosi, and southern Tamaulipas states, where a highly developed tradition of free-standing anthropomorphic figures had flourished throughout the Postclassic period (Fig. 9). Many Mexica statues of this type preserve the ritual gesture of holding the right hand over the breast, a gesture also peculiar to some of the most ancient Huaxtec pieces. But, as happened with so many other borrowed sculptural forms, the artisans of Tenochtitlan were quick to exploit the possibilities of variation; recognizably anthropomorphic cult idols became the basis for such pieces as the colossal Coatlicue, a sculpture representing an aggregate of ritual attire (Fig. 10). Images of such enormous size and weight had not been fashioned in the Central Highlands since the time of Classic Teotihuacan, some 800 years before.

The Pattern of Synthesis at Tenochtitlan

We have seen that a long-established symbolic code stemming from the manuscript tradition found new purposes in Mexica historical commemorative monuments; that figures from a vanished but revered and legendary warrior nation were resuscitated to serve as models for new, but more complex, images for the palaces and temples of Tenochtitlan; and that a genre of cult effigies of probable Huaxtec origin suddenly

Fig. 5 Standing warrior, Mexica (Magali Carrera, personal communication). Photo courtesy of the Museo Nacional de Antropología, Mexico.

Fig. 6 Standing warrior, Mexica. Photo courtesy of the Museo Nacional de Antropología, Mexico.

Fig. 7 Standing "nude" cult effigy, Mexica. Photo courtesy of the Museo Nacional de Antropología, Mexico.

Fig. 8 Attired effigy of Xochipilli, "flower prince." Photo courtesy of the Museo Nacional de Antropología, Mexico.

Fig. 9 Huaxtec cult effigy, *ca.* A.D. 800–900? Compare the ritual gesture with that of the Mexica effigy, Figure 7. Photo courtesy of the Museo Nacional de Antropología, Mexico.

found expanded use at the Mexica capital and neighboring cities. These are only token examples to illustrate a synthesis; they by no means cover the variety of sculpture at Tenochtitlan. Certainly by the 1470s, the decade when the Stone of Tizoc (Fig. 19) was commissioned, Mexica sculpture had attained a stylistic and iconographic integration that is clearly distinguishable in the spectrum of the Mesoamerican arts; a new sculpture had been created whose forms were charged with a dynamic, muscular appearance of great plastic force, the hallmark of the Mexica style.

Scholars generally agree that this pattern is one of renaissance (Nicholson 1971a), but the phenomenon needs fuller qualification if we are to understand the issue of continuity and disjunction. The fact that sculptures executed in the new style have been found in several communities of the southern Valley of Mexico, as well as in the ruins of Tenochtitlan and elsewhere in the Central Highlands and in territories that came under Highland political control, has led to the notion that a widespread renaissance was already underway by the late fourteenth century in such places as Azcapotzalco and Culhuacan. The fact that sculptors were brought from Azcapotzalco to work at Tenochtitlan has already been mentioned. Indeed, the speed with which stylistic and iconographic synthesis was achieved at Tenochtitlan suggests a "pre-Mexica" period of experimentation, though we lack the necessary archaeological proofs. We may certainly conjecture that a basic inventory of traditional themes was in use among the sculptors of the petty fourteenth-century states, yet it is surely appropriate to speak of Tenochtitlan as the epicenter of fifteenth- and early sixteenth-century sculpture, in the same way that one speaks of Florence in relation to other fifteenth-century Italian cities. It is appropriate to distinguish the position and the role of Tenochtitlan in this way, because the prime motivation for putting together an imperial monumental ensemble must have originated largely in the Mexica capital; all the key monuments of the period are from that place, and their iconography, as we shall eventually see, is illustrative of Mexica imperial concerns. This leads to the assump-

Fig. 10 The colossal Coatlicue. Above, front view. Photo courtesy of the Museo Nacional de Antropología, Mexico. Right, side rear view.

tion that it was the Mexica leaders who were primarily concerned with visualizing the need for a powerful new public art, and that it was in the councils of Tenochtitlan that the necessary questions were asked, and the appropriate answers were conceived.

It is informative to compare the situation at Tenochtitlan with the interests of the Islamic culture during its early formative period. Faced with Christian competition, the new Muslim rulers of the Middle East began the development of an assertive series of forms for religious and secular purposes (Grabar 1973). The artistically impoverished Arabian peninsula lacked a major architectural tradition, and it was to the Mediterranean and Iranian arts that invading Muslims turned for a vocabulary of forms from which to choose in the creation of a new, specifically Islamic art. Thus Late Antique, Byzantine, and Sassanian structural and decorative elements were incorporated into a series of early mosques and palaces. However, it took approximately two hundred years for the first hesitant and somewhat mechanically integrated solutions to attain full organic integration and a sense of internal self-sufficiency. It is therefore speculated that it took this length of time to effect a complete change in the vision and the mind of the beholder, whereby a group of signs had become transformed to mean something else. In effect, it was the purpose of this new art to separate forms from their earlier meaning, and to reassemble them in new combinations that were invested with new meaning appropriate to new cultural concerns. But the Mexica synthesis of forms was the last and most visible manifestation of a long process of acculturation whereby a marginal tribe of immigrants had gradually become urban, and had then evolved into an imperial nation with a cosmopolitan capital of unrivaled size and splendor. Stylistic and iconographic synthesis took place with swiftness

at Tenochtitlan because the task was not of the same magnitude as that of early Islam. The Mexica had no confrontation with a powerful competitor state equipped with a rival religious and imperial ideology and a highly evolved art tradition. The artisans of Tenochtitlan incorporated a vocabulary of forms that had widespread circulation, but there was no motivation to bring about a major transformation of meaning such as had taken place in the formation of Islamic art. Despite the innovations that helped to define the unique character and aims of the Mexica imperial state, monumental sculpture at Tenochtitlan was obliged to maintain a fundamental continuity since it had to remain intelligible to all beholders in the cosmopolitan city. A major separation of form and meaning would unnecessarily cloud this purpose.

In examining the Mexica monuments, we will see that it was indispensable for the state to validate itself by representing its indissoluble connection with the sacred universe. It may be hypothesized that this central ideological concern was understood by many peoples, and that it must have had ancient widespread roots throughout the land. This fundamental notion may stem from Classic Maya, Teotihuacan, and Preclassic Olmec cultures. Although it can be conjectured that ideological concerns were similar, in that all these peoples shared a common attitude regarding the cosmos, the actual form that the cosmic symbols took varied with time, place, and the specialized concerns of individual social systems. Much greater variation—and disjunction—occurs with those signs and symbols expressing the unique historical events, economic activities, and social structure of the different Mesoamerican societies. Clearly, the full testing of these notions is a major task for future study; our immediate concern is to begin by establishing the meaning of key monuments in the sculpture of Tenochtitlan.

The Meaning and Function of Cult Effigies

Ritual Attire as a Visual Metaphoric Language

Basically plastic in its character, Mexica art assigned an expanded role to three-dimensional anthropomorphic cult effigies. Several reliable sixteenth-century sources relate that the extensive use of such figures had been a recent phenomenon in the Central Highlands, and that it was specifically associated with Tenochtitlan, Texcoco, and other cities of the southern lake region (Muñoz Camargo 1947: 153; Carrasco 1950: 135). It is almost certain that the custom of using large-scale effigies was originally borrowed from the Huastecs, and was carried out principally at Tenochtitlan and the centers within its immediate sphere of influence. From these places the custom spread elsewhere in the Central Highlands, even to communities and nations in open conflict with the Mexica and their allies.

To an unprecedented degree cult idols proliferated in the monumental ensemble of Tenochtitlan, occupying focal positions in the urban temples and at a multitude of shrines on mountains, at springs, and in sacred groves scattered throughout the surrounding countryside. Few of these effigies have survived in proportion to their numbers, for they were especially singled out for destruction by the Spanish friars, and those not broken up or burnt were secretly buried by the Indians. Basically there are two types of idols. Figures of the first type were carved as "nudes," with only elementary clothing, such as loincloth or mask (Fig. 7). These "nudes" rarely show accurate anatomical proportioning or detail, though the sculptors clearly took a veristic approach to the human form. The vast majority are conventionalized, with only such details as collarbones and articulations of the limbs rendered so as to suggest the internal structure of the body. This relative lack of interest in the human form as such is understandable, for it is virtually a certainty that these "nude" figures were dressed, like mannequins, in ceremonial masks, capes, skirts, jewelry, and other articles of ritual attire. In other words, the clothing could be changed according to the ceremonial occasion. The second type of effigy was carved already fully attired, with extraordinary accuracy and attention given to the detail of ritual garments. The celebrated Xochipilli ("flower prince") figure is a prime example of this type (Fig. 8). Seated with crossed ankles upon an altar-like dais, Xochipilli is shown pasted over with floral and aquatic symbols, some of which are more elaborately repeated on the dais designs. A fanged half-mask hangs over the figure's chest, and the face is covered with another, human mask fitted with an elaborate headdress falling over the shoulders to the middle of the back. Other items —wristbands, armbands, anklets, and knotted sandals —are carved with equal attention to detail. By comparison, the actual physique is generalized and undifferentiated: limbs and extremities have a blocky, rubbery look, without the muscular tension one finds in the Classical and Classicizing sculpture of the Mediterranean world. Actually, these effigies were immobile replicas of ritually costumed personages known to us as impersonators, who appeared as living, moving cult images in the streets and plazas on religious festival occasions. The pictorial screenfold manuscripts illustrate these personages in colorful detail (Fig. 11). It is clear enough that ceremonial costume was the center of interest, and not the human form or individual personality.

There is great variety in the iconography and aesthetic value of such cult idols, but within this variety there are groups of closely related images that especially lend themselves to study. To understand the meaning of ritual attire, it will be particularly useful to describe a series of key figures in one such group, which for the present purpose shall be called the Tlaltecuhtli ("earth lord") series (Figs. 12–14). Perhaps the most interesting single figure in this series was recently unearthed during excavations for the Mexico City

23

Fig. 11 Ritual impersonators. Above, from the Codex Borbonicus, p. 30; below, from the Codex Magliabecchiano, p. 45. Reproduced with the permission of Akademische Druck- u. Verlagsanstalt, Graz, from the facsimile editions.

subway system (Fig. 12). Preoccupation with accurate representation of ritual attire is strikingly illustrated by this image, in which the human form is obscured almost to the point of becoming unrecognizable. But a careful look reveals a pose similar to that of Xochipilli: the figure is seated in cross-legged position with the head thrown sharply back, facing the sky. The hands rest palms-up on, or just in front of, the shoulders, in what is evidently a ritual gesture. A large grotesque mask covering the head faces skywards, and is covered with circular roundels, probably representing precious pieces of jade; an enormous tongue protrudes from grinning teeth; it, too, is ornamented with circular jade pieces, as well as a stylized sacrificial knife. The fearsome visage is framed by circular earplugs and elaborate pendants, and a semicircular tiara holds back the intricately knotted and ornamented hair. A three-strand necklace of beads hides the juncture of the mask with the body of the wearer, and a necklace of severed human hands and hearts is strung across the chest. Hands and forearms are covered with heavy, clawed gloves with striated cuffs, from which strips of paper hang down to the elbows. The legs are similarly covered, and anklets of small metal bells are fitted around the lower legs. Stylized, fanged faces appear at the articulations of the limbs. The bizarre costume is completed by a short skirt covered with skull-and-crossbones designs, secured at the waist by a sash; a circular emblematic device consisting of a stylized human skull with a pendant braided apron is fixed to the small of the back. Similar articles of ritual attire are reproduced in a number of well-known related relief figures of this Tlaltecuhtli series (Figs. 13, 14). It can readily be seen that such images become almost an alphabet of ritual attire. As observed above, it has long been recognized—on the basis of sixteenth-century reports of Sahagún, Durán, Motolinía, and others—that these idols were immobile replicas of the ritual functionaries known as impersonators or deity-substitutes, with the corresponding notion that such effigies and costumed personages acted as representatives of gods and goddesses. But there are rules for using these reports effectively, and the first one is that all the information must be screened: the texts must be examined for the misinterpretations and projections that the Spanish friars naturally and unintentionally made because of their own cultural background. All too frequently the data have been uncritically accepted and then equally uncritically projected back to illuminate some earlier Mesoamerican horizon, compounding error upon error. Such has been the case concerning the meaning of these cult effigies. When the friars first encountered them, they naturally tried to grasp their meaning by referring in their own minds back to the more familiar Mediterranean traditions of idolatrous practices. For example, just as Poseidon was considered to be the ruler of the sea, or Zeus the ruler of the family of gods, so it came to be assumed that the Mexica had a similar pantheon of gods who controlled the forces of nature and human destiny. And so, with this model in mind, it was supposed that ritual attire was emblematic of Mesoamerican gods. Each impersonator was thought to be the substitute or deputy of a god or goddess, as if belonging to a chain of authority that began with a deity and continued, in descending order of importance, with a given natural force such as the earth or rain, followed by an impersonator, then a cult effigy, and, finally, ritual attire. These ideas have become fixed and accepted in the anthropological literature for a very long time and must be seriously questioned. In part, the Spanish were correct: there *is* a connection between the natural forces and ritual paraphernalia; but to the Indian mind, the relationship was more immediate than the Spanish supposed it to be. Fortunately for us, Bernardino de Sahagún took pains to write down the information from his Indian informants in the original Nahuatl language, spoken by the Mexica and other peoples of the Valley. We can therefore turn to the original Nahuatl terminology—the *nomenclature*—of impersonators, cult effigies, and ritual paraphernalia. It is a matter of interpreting these images by retranslating key Nahuatl terms having to do with ancient notions of the sacred, and by understanding a complex metaphoric language by which the phenomena of nature were described.

25

Fig. 12 First cult figure of the Tlaltecuhtli series, front and top view (above) and rear view (left). The rear view shows the characteristic skull emblem and plaited pendant at small of the back. Note elaborately knotted hair falling down across the shoulders. Photos courtesy of the Museo Nacional de Antropología, Mexico.

Fig. 13 Relief figure from the Tlaltecuhtli series. Compare with Figure 12, rear view; note skull with pendant at small of the back. The mask is upside-down to indicate the sky-ward-facing ritual position. Photo courtesy of the Museo Nacional de Antropología, Mexico.

Fig. 14 Another relief figure from the Tlaltecuhtli series. Here the upside-down mask is architectonically stylized, with a row of rounded teeth protruding from a gaping, cornice-like mouth (extreme top). The eyes are represented directly below this mouth, with elaborately curling eyebrows. Knotted hair falls across the shoulders. A large circular diadem, thought to signify the "navel of the earth," has been substituted for the skull and pendant; the skull-and-crossbones skirt design appears on a panel set between the crouching legs. Note clawed extremities. Photo courtesy of the Museo Nacional de Antropología, Mexico.

Words such as "impersonator" or "substitute" are only approximate translations of the Nahuatl term *teixiptla*. In the Nahuatl texts, *teixiptla* is used not only to describe living, moving cult performers (costumed persons), but also effigies of stone, wood, dough, or simply *any* assemblage of ritual attire on a wooden frame that included a mask (Hvidtfeldt 1958). All of these things were categorized in the same way, and had equivalent representational value in the Indian mind. Living impersonators, effigies, or ritual attire assembled upon a frame were all *teixiptla*, with no particular notion of descending order of rank. What did all these things represent?

It is questionable that they represented gods in any conventional sense of the term. What they were connected with was designated in two ways: first, by the word *teotl*, and, second, by a metaphoric cult name describing natural phenomena or the attributes of a revered tribal ancestral hero. There are frequent occasions in which *teotl* and the metaphoric cult name are mentioned in the same context, a fact that makes it apparent that one term qualifies the other (Hvidtfeldt 1958). *Teotl* was universally translated by the Spanish as "god," "saint," or sometimes "demon," but its actual meaning more closely corresponds with that of the Polynesian term *mana*, signifying a numinous, impersonal force diffused throughout the universe. This force was preeminently manifested in the natural forces—earth, air, fire, and water—but was also to be found in persons of great distinction, or things and places of unusual or mysterious configuration. *Teotl* expresses the notion of sacred quality, but with the idea that it could be physically manifested in some specific presence—a rainstorm, a mirage, a lake, or a majestic mountain. It is as if the world was perceived as being magically charged, inherently alive in greater or lesser degree with this vital force. Everything in the world was potentially a hierophany: things, animals, people, transitory phenomena had the capacity to manifest some aspect of the sacred. And for ritual purposes, of course, a *teixiptla* especially acted as a talismanic token of the sacred.

Next to be examined are the metaphoric cult names

of natural phenomena and ancestral tribal heroes. First we shall be concerned with natural phenomena, leaving the question of heroes to be taken up in the second half of the present chapter. The metaphoric cult names were regarded by the Spanish as the specific names of gods and goddesses. But in fact they do not seem to describe supernatural personages as much as they seem *directly to describe natural phenomena*, period, without the idea of an intermediary god or goddess. This is best illustrated in Nahuatl poetry, the language of ceremonial situations. Nahuatl poetry routinely used highly metaphoric language which is remarkably akin to the *kennings* of Old Norse poetry of the thirteenth century (see Rowe 1962: 15 for a discussion of *kennings* as a probable key to Chavín iconography in Peru). To give an example of a kenning, if we say "the lake's water is like jade," we are making a simile or direct comparison; if we say "the lake's jade water," we are making an implied comparison, or metaphor, not likening the water to jade, but calling it jade; however, if we say "she of the skirt of jade," without mentioning either the lake or the water, then we are making a comparison by substitution, or kenning: the lake is personalized as "she" and the water is a "skirt of jade." Kennings are an extended form of metaphor, in which, to understand the meaning, the listener must share with the speaker the knowledge that in ceremonial or courtly language it is customary to refer to the water of lakes as skirts of jade. As the taste for kennings developed in Old Norse court poetry, bards devised kennings of kennings, and kennings which depended on a story which the listeners were assumed to know. Nahuatl poetry abounds in similar conceits, many of which have been recently analyzed (León-Portilla 1963; Martínez 1972).

Thus Tenochtitlan was also variously known as "the place where darts were made," "the place of the white willows," or "the place of the eagle and the cactus"; warfare or battle was "the song of shields," "where the smoke of shields diffuses," or "flowers of the heart upon the plain"; the place where poetry was composed was "the house of spring," "the flowery patio," or "the bower of flowers" (Martínez 1972:

126–9). Natural phenomena were similarly described in metaphoric terms. The earth was ritually addressed as Tlalli yiollo, "heart of the earth"; Toci, "our grandmother"; or Teteo innan, "mother of the gods" (teotl) (Sahagún 1951–1970, Bk. 1: 15). Such titles have a personalizing tendency but this need not imply, as it traditionally has, that a god or goddess with a life of its own is the subject of the address. Rather, we may interpret "mother" and "grandmother" as allusions to the procreative and sustaining qualities of the earth. Tlalli yiollo has a related meaning as the conceptualized locus of the earth's life force. Similarly the title Tlaltecuhtli, "earth lord," was an honorific title (Durán 1971: 261). Still other names allude to the earth's receptive role in confessional rites—an extension of the earth's receptive position in the cosmic order—as with Tlazolteotl, "sacred eater of filth":

... As to her being named Tlaçolteotl: it was said that it was because her realm, her domain, was that of evil and perverseness—that is to say, lustful and debauched living. It was said that she ruled and was mistress of lust and debauchery. (Sahagún 1951–70, Bk. 1: 23)

Another title, Tlaelquani, is similarly explained:

And as for her being called Tlaelquani: it was said it was because one told, one recited before her, all vanities; one told, one spread before her, all unclean works—however ugly, however grave; avoiding nothing because of shame. Indeed, all was exposed, told before her. (Sahagún 1951–70, Bk. 1: 23)

Linking various names and titles for the same subject within a single text was a descriptive device to portray different aspects or attributes, as in the (abbreviated) Song of Teteo innan:

The yellow flower hath opened—she, our mother with the thigh skin of the goddess painted on her face, departed from Tamoanchan.
. . . .
The white flower hath blossomed—she, our mother with the thigh skin of the goddess painted on her face, departed from Tamoanchan.
. . . .
She hath become a goddess, upon the melon cactus, our mother Itzpapalotl.

Thou hast seen the nine dry plains, the deer's heart upon which was fed our mother Tlaltecuhtli.
Once again with chalk, with feathers is she pasted. In the four directions hath the arrow shattered. . . .(Sahagún 1951–70, Bk. 2: 208–9).

Thus Teteo innan, "mother of the sacred spirit," is also Itzpapalotl, "obsidian butterfly," and (tonan) Tlaltecuhtli, "our mother earth-lord" (lady). If each of these metaphoric titles were taken as the proper name of a distinct deity, it would be impossible to find the subject of the poem. Metaphors for the earth were also created with earth-associated animals, as in Coatlicue, "serpent skirt"; still other passages describe Tlaltecuhtli, "earth lord," as a crouching, froglike creature with clawed extremities and a gaping, tooth-studded mouth, and with additional mouths at the elbows and knees, all intended to describe the voracious, inevitably all-consuming position of the earth towards all that grows and moves upon its surface (Mendieta 1945, 1: 87; Histoyre du Méchique 1905). By taking all such names as the names of gods and goddesses, the Spanish arrived at the conclusion that there existed some kind of endlessly proliferating pantheon of interrelated and interpenetrating deities, a notion that has persisted down to the present day. In reality, we are confronted simply with a litany of kennings describing aspects of the same phenomenon.

Our remaining task is to connect kennings with ritual attire, specifically to the attire of the figures in our Tlaltecuhtli series, which may serve as an example of the general pattern. It was the function of ritual attire to express visually these metaphoric cult names: it can be called a visual metaphoric language. The froglike conception of the earth, called Tlaltecuhtli (see also Nicholson 1967: 83–8), is the basis for the grotesque teixiptlas with clawed hands, grinning teeth, and snapping mouths at the articulations of the limbs (Figs. 12–14). Items of ritual attire are descriptive of cosmic phenomena, not of the personality of an anthropomorphic god. Just as various descriptive titles or names were combined in a given song or poetic address, so also there are exchanges, borrowings, and different combinations of ritual attire from figure to figure.

Fig. 15 Small Coatlicue, combining pictographic skirt with clawed extremities and skull otherwise worn by figures of the Tlaltecuhtli series. Compare also with the colossal Coatlicue, Figure 10. Photo courtesy of the Museo Nacional de Antropología, Mexico.

This is clearly illustrated by the pictographic skirt *coatlicue*, "serpent skirt," used in combination with the clawed gloves and moccasins otherwise worn by Tlaltecuhtli (Fig. 15); note also how this figure wears the skull as a mask, instead of as a device fixed at the small of the back. This Coatlicue effigy is a visual metaphor for the earth as it was conceived in terms of female procreative and destructive qualities. Certainly the most celebrated monument exhibiting these characteristics is the colossal Coatlicue, an idol which can be called anthropomorphic only in a general structural sense, as it is primarily an assemblage of ritual attire from various related sources (Fig. 10). Here again we encounter the skirt of interwoven serpents, the skull-and-apron plaited device at the small of the back, the fanged faces at the elbows, the clawed feet, and the sacrificial necklace of hands and hearts. The figure also wears a human female skin, which was a common symbol of regeneration (when worn by a human *teixiptla*, such dried skins were likened to a husk enclosing a living seed). Male aspects of the earth are indicated by the serpent-headed loincloth-end appearing between the figure's legs. Finally, the dual serpents rising from the torso to confront each other seem not to be a mask but an allusion to the blood of sacrifice by decapitation (Fernández 1954).

As visual metaphors, these examples of *teixiptlas* from the Tlaltecuhtli series portrayed the earth not as it was seen by the physical eye, but as it was conceived in terms of a spectrum of life-forces. The Spanish friars equated Nahuatl metaphors for the earth and other natural phenomena with the ancient Greek gods and goddesses, without taking into account unfamiliar notions of the sacred and the abstruse conventions of poetic discourse. But there is a rainbowlike quality to these supposed gods of Mesoamerica; the closer one searches for a personal identity so vividly displayed by the anthropomorphic deities of the Mediterranean world, the more evanescent and immaterial they become, dissolved in mists of allusion and allegory with which Mexica poets and sculptors expressed their sense of the miraculous in the world about them. It seems therefore reasonable to speak of an essentially nontheistic manner of perceiving the universe as hallowed, and of a society that institutionalized its relationship to the universe through cults addressed to natural phenomena. We have described a few figures from the Tlaltecuhtli series, pertaining to the earth cult; but there are many other figures to be examined in future studies: these pertain to the cult of rain, moisture, and aquatic phenomena; to the cult of fire and solar heat; to the cult of wind, or air; and so forth. In the political fragmentation of Late Postclassic times, different sociopolitical groups had evolved localized versions of these major cult themes, which helps to account for the diversity of metaphoric images describing the same phenomenon. Logically it was in metropolitan Tenochtitlan, where a multiplicity of peoples from different provinces coexisted and maintained their own ceremonial life, that we find such variety and interplay between essentially related images. We shall find out on the following pages that each community within the city—various professional groups from all levels of society—was responsible for at least one ceremony or an aspect of some major festival dedicated to a cosmic theme in the recurring yearly cycle. Under these conditions, the special interests of the state influenced the tenor of ceremonialism; among the warlike Mexica, the impersonators and cult idols acquired a distinctly bloodthirsty quality, as abundant sacrificial motifs reflected a preoccupation with violent death. Added to this was an overriding concern for political and ideological integration, with the corresponding creation of such images as the compound, colossal Coatlicue, which expresses the earth-cult theme in terms reflecting the synthesizing preoccupations of the Mexica nation.

Cult Effigies and the Commemoration of Community Ancestors

The cult effigies that manifested the sacred aspects of the universe also commemorated deceased tribal magnates, and the relationship of these magnates with the cosmic forces. In assuming responsibility for the biological and cultural existence of a community, leaders were charged with the responsibility of maintaining a harmonious relationship with the cosmos through religious obligations, which included direct personal participation as impersonators or the sponsoring of impersonation. In this capacity, rulers from the level of clan chieftains, the representatives of professional groups, and the kings of extensive states assumed a hallowed status and, during ceremonial time, attained a position of virtual interchangeability with the *teotl* of a natural phenomenon. The death of a ruler was commemorated by fashioning a ceremonially attired cult effigy—a *teixiptla*—which ritually affirmed his or her assimilation to that phenomenon or force. Placed in the urban temples and at many shrines scattered throughout the tribal lands, these *teixiptlas* reminded the community that the worship of the natural elements was inseparably connected with the memory of the deceased; indeed, *teixiptlas* affirmed a traditional and continuing tutelary relationship between venerated magnates and their people. But here again it must be borne in mind that it was not a *personality* that was being commemorated but, rather, the *continuing office of leaders* in preserving a transcendental affinity between the cosmic and the social orders.

Community leaders and impersonation

At Tenochtitlan, where sanguinary cult practices were greatly emphasized as a general policy aimed at inuring the population to violence and bloodshed as a way of life, it had become customary to sacrifice impersonators at the conclusion of ceremonial activities. Consequently, the magnates rarely performed impersonation themselves. Instead, they ordinarily purchased slaves to fulfill that purpose, as shown, for example, in Sahagún's description of the traders' rites held annually at Tenochtitlan during the Panquetzalitztli festivals (Sahagún 1951–70, Bk. 9: 45–67). The rites were initiated by young traders wishing to consecrate themselves in their profession, as if they were postulants or neophytes in a religious order. The first act was to purchase slaves in the marketplace at Azcapotzalco; then the group made a long pilgrimage to

Tochtepec, where the great southern trade route leading from the Central Highlands split, one branch leading down into Oaxaca, the Isthmus of Tehuantepec, and the Pacific coastal plain of Guatemala, the other to the Gulf Coast and Yucatán. Colonies of traders from the Central Highlands were established at Tochtepec, where, before the traders' idol Yiacatecuhtli, the young aspiring traders first displayed the ritual attire that was to be worn later by the purchased slaves at Tenochtitlan. After receiving the wise admonitions of the elder resident traders, the neophytes packed away the now-sanctified attire for the return trip to Tenochtitlan. Upon returning, these men ritually bathed the slaves and then arrayed them and bade them dance; and then, after numerous ceremonies and feasts, the impersonators were conducted through the city to the shrine of Huitzilopochtli for their sacrificial demise. As a concluding act, the now-confirmed traders were presented with the ritual attire of their deceased impersonators for safekeeping through the remainder of their lives:

He . . . who bathed slaves, for as long as he still lived on earth, always guarded his sacred reed box. There he kept what had been the array of his bathed slave, all his adornment, all that has been mentioned: the cape, the breech clout, the sandals, the skirt, the shift, everything. Nothing was omitted; verily, all he guarded for himself. Indeed all the hair from the crowns of [the slave's] heads he packed into the sacred reed box. And later, if the bather of the slaves died, they burned [all this] for him. (Sahagún 1951–70, Bk. 9: 67)

Here the talismanic association of ritual attire with the future leaders of a hereditary professional group is clearly demonstrated. Similar instances are indicated among other communities within the city, as in the case of those who worked with water, who annually sacrificed a Chalchihuitlicue ("she of the jade skirt") impersonator at the Tlaloc shrine, which was located next to that of Huitzilopochtli atop the Main Pyramid of Tenochtitlan:

And right before her image died a woman slave whom they had bought. The water merchants exhibited her; those who gained their livelihoods from water, those who brought water in boats, those who owned boats, those who lived on the water, the boatmakers, those who served water in the market place.

Likewise they arrayed her, made offerings, and ornamented her; for she would go, when she died, to a place called Tlalocan. . . .
. . . .

. . . [for] they remembered that because of her we live. She is our sustenance. And thence come all things that are necessary. (Sahagún 1951–70, Bk. 1: 22)

This pattern is repeated on the highest social levels, as when the Emperor himself arrayed the Tezcatlipoca ("smoking mirror") impersonator during the annual Toxcatl festivals (the significance of Tezcatlipoca will be discussed on following pages). Yet even at Tenochtitlan there were still instances of direct impersonation performed by great Mexica magnates, as when Prince Cihuacoatl, the governor of the city, wore Cihuacoatl ("serpent-woman," another earth-cult variant) attire to welcome the Emperor Moctezuma Xocoyotzin upon his triumphant return from the Quezaltepec campaign (Durán 1964: 230). Similarly, the great lords were ritually attired upon departing for the wars (Sahagún 1951–70, Bk. 8: 33–5); for instance, the Emperor Ahuizotl adopted Xipe Totec costume as his battle-dress, and was so portrayed in his commemorative funerary image, carved in relief upon the cliffs at Chapultepec. The dried human skin worn by Xipe Totec ("flayed lord") impersonators had the same symbolic function as that appearing on the colossal Coatlicue; it seems likely that in adopting this costume Ahuizotl intended to draw parallels between a well-known image of springtime regeneration and his role as the creator of a new political order in the conquered lands of Mesoamerica.

Cult effigies as commemorative funerary monuments

The use of *teixiptlas* in funerary contexts spelled out the continuing connections of community leaders with the cosmic forces. In describing the funeral of the Emperor Axayacatl, Durán gives us the following account:

. . . A great bower was prepared; this was called *tlacochcalli*, which means "house of repose." Within the bower was placed a statue which was the image of the dead king. The figure was made of slivers of wood bound together. Its face imitated that of a human being, its head was feathered with plumes called *ichcacaxochitl*, "cotton flowers," and others called *malacaquetzalli*, "spindle-whorl feathers," together with a breastplate of feather work. He was then dressed in the splendid garments worn by the god Huitzilopochtli. Over this garb he was dressed with the garments of the divinity Tlaloc so that he represented that deity. . . . The fourth garment he wore was that of the god Yohualahua. . . . The fifth attire was that of the deity Quetzalcoatl. On his head they placed a mask in the form of a jaguar with a goose-like beak. Since he was the god of the wind he wore light clothing in the form of wings with rounded edges and a loincloth with rounded borders together with a small mantle called Butterfly Mantle. (Durán 1964: 176–7)

In the conclusion of the ritual, this composite bundle was placed together with the body of the deceased emperor upon a pyre in front of the Huitzilopochtli idol, and both were burned. Although Durán phrases his account in terms of "gods," we may recognize that what is happening is that a *teixiptla* of the emperor is dressed in clothing expressing his identity with natural forces or certain great ancestral leaders of hallowed memory (the latter will be discussed in the next section of this chapter). The fact that the ancestral dead were considered to be assimilated to the cosmos was recorded not only at Tenochtitlan, but elsewhere throughout the Central Highlands: "To all their dead they gave the name *teotl* so-and-so, which means 'god so-and-so' or 'saint so-and-so'," writes Sahagún's great contemporary Motolinía, who was especially familiar with the beliefs and practices of Tlaxcala (Motolinía 1951: 106). Torquemada, also summarizing Tlaxcalan customs, noted the connection between these venerated ancestors and the use of cult effigies:

. . . they gave the status of divinity to their dead kings and to all those outstanding persons who had died bravely in the wars and as captives of their enemies; and they made idols of them and they placed them with their gods, saying they had departed to the place of amusements and delights in the company of other gods. (Carrasco 1950: 141–2)

A final and extremely significant observation on Tlaxcalan customs was made by Motolinía, who remarked

that such *teixiptlas* were not only distributed in urban temples, but also in shrines scattered throughout tribal territory:

. . . The idols, of which the Indians had very many, were set up in . . . conspicuous places, as in groves and on prominent hills and especially mountain passes and summits; in short, wherever there was a high spot or a place inviting to repose by reason of its loveliness . . .

They also had idols near the water, chiefly at the outlet of springs, where they set up their altars with the roofed stairway. At many of the principal springs . . . they had four such altars, placed in the form of a cross, one in front of the other and one on either side, with the spring in the center. . . . Also around large trees, like cypresses and cedars, they erected such altars and offered the same sacrifices. . . . (Motolinía 1951: 107)

Durán also notes that idols were commonly placed in caves, especially within those of the most venerated mountain peaks of the Central Highlands (Durán 1971: 248–60). The most conspicuous shrine with these characteristics in the immediate vicinity of Tenochtitlan was at the hill of Chapultepec, with its abundant fresh water springs and its groups of immense cypresses and cedars. A temple occupied the summit of this hill, where Maximilian's Chapultepec Palace stands today, and, at the time the Spanish first visited the site, a host of idols virtually covered the cool and shaded space beneath the trees. It was upon the cliff of this hill, close to the imperial capital, that the funerary images of the Mexica emperors were carved, though these exist in the most fragmentary form today and their original appearance must be reconstructed from original eyewitness accounts (Nicholson 1961). Could these sculptural reliefs be considered categorically different from the free-standing *teixiptlas*? The distinction is difficult to make. The royal relief-sculptures clearly commemorate specific individuals. They are not as anonymous, as collective, as abstractly identified with the ritual offices of community leadership as are the images of impersonators. But they must surely represent another facet of the same phenomenon, as royal personages were depicted clad in the kind of ritual attire (Xipe Totec) also worn by ceremonial impersonators.

33

Throughout Central Highland Mexico, the great notables who personified their respective communities were sanctified by virtue of their associations with the life forces of the universe. But here again we cannot properly speak of gods, because of the primacy of nature in lending these notables their posthumous animation and significance. It was the function of the visual metaphoric language of *teixiptlas* to express this primacy. *Teixiptlas* did not primarily advertise a personality, though the reliefs of emperors and kings were doubtlessly accompanied by dates and name-glyphs; rather, *teixiptlas* commemorated a lasting relationship between a community—personified by its leader—and the animating spirits of the universe. Individual identity seems more directly connected with social identity, with social function, than with personal psyche. Distributed in shrines throughout the urban sphere and the surrounding countryside, cult effigies validated the social order by reminding the population of their ancestral dead and the communion of the group with a larger universal order.

Great founder-leaders and the political significance of teixiptlas

Just as every clan or professional group within a nation had its canonized ancestral leader or sequence of leaders who maintained the group's connections with the supernatural, so the nation as a whole, on a grander scale, had a great patron at its head, an ancestral founder-leader who figured importantly in the nation's history. In the politically fragmented situation existing in the Central Highlands before the triple alliance of Tenochtitlan, Texcoco, and Tlacopan, each nation had evolved its own political and religious orthodoxy centered around the cult of their respective tutelary patrons. This pattern was discerned by Carrasco in reviewing the sixteenth-century sources on the Otomí. Drawing comparisons with the Tepanec, Matlazinca, and Tlaxcalan peoples, Carrasco noted that the Otomí tribal patron, Otontecuhtli, had probably originally been a leader—or the name given to a succession of leaders—who in death had become the

focus of a cult assimilated to that of Old Father, the Otomí conceptualization of the primordial male creative principle. "One of the main processes by which Mesoamerican religions produce such great quantities of deities is the deification of an ancestral tribal leader, who assumes the attributes of the gods of the tribe he represents," concluded Carrasco (1950: 143), phrasing his observations in terms of standard notions concerning the existence of a pantheon of gods. Thus each nation within the Central Highlands maintained a sense of individuality and unity through commemoration of ancestral personages whose identity was inseparably associated with a given natural force.

The most powerful states offered elaborate cults to their great patron-founders. Tezcatlipoca was associated with the prestigious city of Texcoco, capital of the old Acolhua domain and the foremost center of learning and the preservation of ancient Mesoamerican tradition in the Valley; Mixcoatl-Camaxtli was revered especially in regions adjacent to Tlaxcala; Quetzalcoatl was preeminently enshrined at Chollolan, the ancient trading city and religious center of the Valley of Puebla; and Huitzilopochtli was the Mexica national patron *par excellence*. The *teixiptlas* and ritual accoutrements of these foremost personages were housed in the principal temples of their respective national capitals.

Alliances between states were affirmed through the exchange of cult effigies. At Tenochtitlan, the images of Tezcatlipoca and Huitzilopochtli were placed side by side in the shrine of the Tlatelolco pyramid, where the Spanish viewed them in the company of Moctezuma. Bernal Díaz del Castillo, who, as we recall, was with the party of Cortés on that occasion, vividly describes the bizarre and stupefying scene as the Spanish visitors were ushered into the darkened temple.

. . . the first, which was on the right-hand side, they said was of Huitzilopochtli, their god of war; and he had a very broad face with deformed and frightening eyes, with the body all covered with a mosaic of stone, gold, and pearls . . . and the body was girdled by something like large serpents of gold and mosaic, and in one hand he held a bow and in the other some arrows . . . He had at his neck the faces of some Indians and other things like the hearts of the same

Indians, and these were of gold and those were of silver with many blue stones; and there were some braziers with incense —that is, copal—and three hearts of Indians which had been sacrificed that day . . . then we saw in another part on the left-hand side another great statue of the height of Huitzilopochtli, and it had a bearlike face and eyes that reflected . . . and its body was covered with mosaics like that of Huitzilopochtli, because they said they were brothers between them; and this Tezcatlipoca was the god of hell, . . . and he had about his body figures like little demons and serpentlike tails; and there was so much blood encrusted on the walls and the floor was bathed in it. . . . (Díaz del Castillo 1904, I: 291–2; author's translation)

Of all the numinous ancestral founder-leaders venerated at the time of the Spanish conquest, Tezcatlipoca was perhaps the most awesome and prestigious. Only the barest traces of the historical identity of this ancient personage can be gleaned from the literary sources. By the time the name Tezcatlipoca (or the synonym Titlacauan) appears in reference to a shamanistic figure in the legendary ideological struggle with Quetzalcoatl of Tollan (Tula), it probably already indicated a cult and a political faction rather than a personality. In any case, the cult as it existed at Texcoco still retained echoes of an archaic, shamanic origin among the tribesmen of the north, embodied principally in a revered obsidian mirror, a magical artifact shamanistically used for divinatory scrying. Enshrined with a Tezcatlipoca cult effigy at Texcoco, this mirror was a talisman whose smoky depths could be contemplated for oracular guidance. Indeed, it was said that in remote times Tezcatlipoca spoke to the Acolhua tribe through this mystic device, during their migration to the Valley of Mexico (Pomar 1964: 159–61). But, in the acculturation process at Texcoco, the Tezcatlipoca cult appears to have been assimilated with a still-earlier cult of urban Mesoamerica; this is revealed in the use of certain metaphoric terms which modern Nahuatl scholars believe were handed down from an antique civilizing tradition (Martínez 1972: 80–5). Thus, in ritual texts, Tezcatlipoca was addressed as Tlacatle Totecoe, meaning "master, lord," an expression of omnipotence; Tloque Nahuaque, "lord of the near and that contained within the circuit," ex-

pressing the notion of an omnipotent presence closest to our being, governing all within the boundaries of the cosmos; Ipalnemoani, "thou by whom we live," referring to the animating principle of the universe; Toalle, "night," and Ehecatl, "wind," both of which convey ideas of invisibility and intangibility; and finally, Moyocoyotzin, "the inventor of himself," a reference to spontaneous creativity (see Sahagún 1951–70, Bk. 6: 1–5; León-Portilla 1963: 89–95; Martínez 1972: 112–5, 125). All these metaphors express the synthesis of an ancient tribal ancestral cult with the cult of the universal creative principle. Indeed, the Tezcatlipoca cult at Texcoco had a distinctly civilizing tone and was devoid of the barbaric practice of human sacrifice that it acquired in Mexica hands. The sixteenth-century texts reveal that the Tezcatlipoca cult was especially connected with the royal house of Texcoco. When Nezahualcoyotl assumed the office of Acolhua Tecuhtli ("lord of Acolhuacan," i.e., king) in 1431, his confirmation rites took place at the Tezcatlipoca shrine and were witnessed by all the magnates of the land, including the monarchs of Tlacopan and Tenochtitlan. Standing in front of the idol and its associated paraphernalia, Nezahualcoyotl shed the blue garments he was wearing and, naked, proceeded to cense the effigy and the cardinal directions; following this he began a solemn and measured address stating the need for the kingdom to conform to the "worship of the ancient god, the father of all the gods, who is the god of fire, who is in the water pool, among battlements surrounded by roselike rocks, he who is named Xiuhtecutli ["turquoise prince"], who determines, examines, and concludes the business and litigation of the people . . ." (Martínez 1972: 25; author's translation). Further on, Tezcatlipoca was petitioned:

Have the goodness to grant me a little light,
Though it be no more than that of a firefly in the night,
To go forth in this dream and this life of sleep,
Which lasts but the space of a day
Where there are many things upon which to stumble,
And many others that occasion us to laugh,
And others still which are like unto a stony path

Along which one must pass by leaping . . .
(Martínez 1972: 26; author's translation)

Such passages disclose the fusion of Tezcatlipoca with an omnipresent and omnipotent creative force diffused throughout the cosmos, and the cult obligation which Nezahualcoyotl had in maintaining the connection between his nation and this animating power.

Needless to say, it was of singular importance for the warlike Mexica to secure the support of this august patron of the Acolhua, but, in placing Tezcatlipoca's *teixiptla* next to that of their own tribal patron, Huitzilopochtli, an appalling transformation in the nature of the cult was carried out in keeping with their own sanguinary imperial state and expansionistic territorial ambitions. Transformations were reciprocal, however, and, in the process of exchange, Huitzilopochtli began to be magnified in metaphoric terms evocative of celestial omnipotence and grandeur. Thus he was addressed as "the blue heron bird," "the lucid macaw," or "the precious heron" (Martínez 1972: 114–5, 125, 196); and, in keeping with these celestial associations, cult idols of Huitzilopochtli were covered with blue turquoise mosaics, or were painted blue, or were depicted seated in a blue bower, or were adorned with blue cotinga-feather earplugs. At the same time Huitzilopochtli's preeminently warlike associations were conveyed by such metaphors as "the eagle" or "the bird of darts" (Díaz del Castillo 1904, I: 291–2). In keeping with the latter associations, his *teixiptla* was equipped with bow and arrows, as Bernal Díaz del Castillo faithfully recounts. But the sacrificial tone of Huitzilopochtli's cult with its corresponding political implications was not regarded sympathetically at Texcoco. Indeed, the installation of his image in a new temple at that city was passively resisted and became the focus of a bitter iconoclastic controversy led by Nezahualcoyotl, who, renouncing the use of cult idols, reasserted the ideal of Tloque Nahuaque and commissioned a new temple without an idol to be built facing the intrusive Mexica shrine.

Nezahualcoyotl's acts point out the degree to which cult idols had become symbols of national identity by the middle of the fifteenth century in Central Highland Mexico. Just as political alliances were celebrated by the mutual exchange of effigies, the conquest of a city or a nation was symbolically affirmed by burning its central temple and carrying away its patron *teixiptla* and ritual paraphernalia into captivity. At Tenochtitlan, a special temple known as the *coateocalli* had been constructed in the main ceremonial precinct to house the captured cult effigies and ritual paraphernalia brought home by triumphantly returning Mexica armies. The importance of this temple was underlined by the fact that it had been commissioned by Moctezuma Xocoyotzin, who personally officiated at the dedication. The *coateocalli* not only served to display captive idols as military trophies, but also acted as a repository for images embodying the identity of defeated nations throughout the land.

Cosmic Symbols and Commemorative Monuments

While anthropomorphic cult effigies expressed the vital bonds between natural forces, ancestors, and living sovereigns and magnates of the nation, another category of sculptural monuments commemorated outstanding historical events as they had actually happened, or, more often, as they were reinterpreted at Tenochtitlan to accord with imperial aspirations. Cosmic symbols were regularly used on such monuments to represent the settings for historical scenes. The organization of these compositions suggests that the inhabitants of Tenochtitlan automatically perceived their city as the center of the world, beyond whose sphere of influence lay chaos—the unconsecrated territory of foreign nations. The pattern of vital affinity between the natural and the social orders is completed by this kind of structural equation between cosmos and state. Any interpretation of Mexica commemorative sculpture must therefore begin with an account of certain basic notions concerning the spatial organization of the universe as it was traditionally conceived among the peoples of the Central Highlands.

Cosmology

Minor variations appear in written accounts of the structure of the universe, but, generally speaking, the earth was seen as a great disc floating in a circumscribing sea, which was thought to rise at the horizon to merge with the lowest level of the heavenly planes (Nicholson 1971b: 403; León-Portilla 1963: 53ff.). We have already seen how the properties of the earth were metaphorically represented and described in discussing the Tlaltecuhtli series. The term cipactli, "alligator," was also sometimes used in this respect: the alligator's ridged back protruding from the water, as seen in coastal swamps, was taken as an image for the mountains and valleys of the land. Four directions extended to the cardinal points from the center, or navel, of the earth's surface. These cosmic quadrants were usually described from a dominant position determined by the path of the sun. The east, the place of the sun's emergence, was pre-eminently the place of life, fertility, and light, and it was assigned the color white (there is much variation in directional colors). The west was the home of the sun, the place of its setting, the land of the red color. The south lay to the left of the sun's path, and was regarded as the quadrant of the color blue. The north was considered unfavorable; lying to the right of the sun, it was assigned the color black. Some sources describe four great cosmic trees growing at the cardinal points, and others identify four Atlaslike sky-bearers occupying the intercardinal positions. There was also a tradition, more prevalent among the Maya peoples and in the Mixteca than in the Valley of Mexico, concerning a central cosmic tree, the *axis mundi*, growing from the navel of the earth to the highest place of the celestial sphere. In the southern Mesoamerican traditions this cosmic tree was often spoken of as a ceiba (*bombax ceiba* in Linnaeus' classification), the towering and majestic tree equated with the primordial source of life (Villa Rojas 1968). The axial relationship between the center of the earth and the celestial sphere was described in essentially related terms by the Central Highlands peoples, who visualized the stratified dome of heaven rising above the land in a succession of levels respectively traversed by the sun, the moon, and the stars, Venus, and the comets; above everything and directly centered over the navel of the earth was Omeyocan, "the place of duality," locus of the self-generated male-female source of life. We have already encountered other figurative terms for the dual principle of this place: Ometeotl, "two sacred spirit," or Ometecuhtli and Omecihuatl, "two lord" and "two lady," etc. These figures of speech correspond in their most essential meaning with Ipalnemoani, "thou by whom we live," and Tloque Nahuaque, "lord of the near, and of that which is contained within the ring

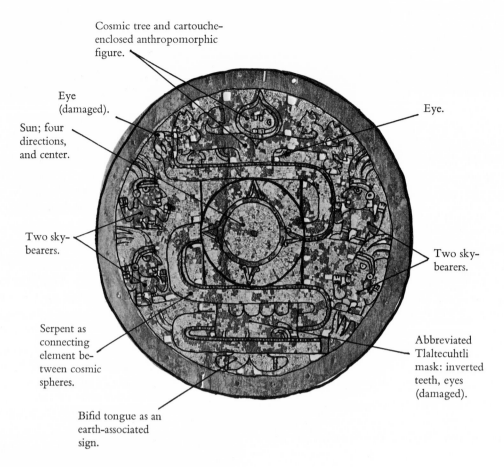

Cosmic tree and cartouche-enclosed anthropomorphic figure.

Eye (damaged).

Sun; four directions, and center.

Eye.

Two sky-bearers.

Two sky-bearers.

Serpent as connecting element between cosmic spheres.

Abbreviated Tlaltecuhtli mask: inverted teeth, eyes (damaged).

Bifid tongue as an earth-associated sign.

Fig. 16 Above, mosaic shield: a cosmogram (after Saville 1922: Pl. xx). Left, an inverted mask showing the same manner of representing teeth (after Saville 1922: Pl. v). Compare with the teeth of the upside-down mask of Tlaltecuhtli, Figure 13. Both objects, British Museum.

or circuit." Mictlan, the "land of the dead," extended below the surface of the earth in a well-defined series of levels which complemented the stratification of the heavens. Like the heavens, the earth was considered to have a locus of procreative vitality, spoken of as Tlalli yiollo, "the heart of the earth."

These vertical and horizontal divisions of cosmic space are represented in simplified and abbreviated form on a ceremonial mosaic shield, now in the collection of the British Museum (Fig. 16). It is thought that this badly damaged though still-brilliant device may have been included in the original booty sent by Cortés to Charles V in 1519. The first drawing of this shield was published in 1895, and Saville later described its history in European collections without attempting an interpretation of the iconography. It was recently published in color in a booklet illustrating all the Mesoamerican mosaics in the British Museum (Carmichael 1970: Frontispiece; see also Read 1895; Saville 1922: Pl. xx). Like most examples of late Postclassic lapidary work, it is attributed to Mixtec craftsmanship; a colony of Mixtec craftsmen resided at Tenochtitlan where they not only practiced their trade but also acted as instructors. Only the greatest of the magnates were privileged to bear these shields in the spectacular dances and processions attended by the lords of Tenochtitlan.

The horizontal division of space corresponding to the surface of the earth is represented by the disc shape of the shield; four anthropomorphic sky-bearers are placed at the intercardinal points of this "horizontal" plane, which is tilted in the composition so as to form the background for an arrangement of motifs describing vertical space. The vertical sequence begins below with a serpent-tongue, followed by an abbreviated Tlaltecuhtli mask. The mask is easily recognized by its characteristic teeth, which are the most indispensable elements of the metaphoric image. The fact that they indeed are teeth may be confirmed by comparing their outline with the teeth of other mosaic masks (Fig. 16). But their position is naturally reversed to conform iconographically with the upward-facing open mouth characteristic of all Tlaltecuhtli images

(compare with Figs. 12, 13, 14). The mouth is, of course, a symbolic entrance to the world below the surface of the earth.

The center of the shield is occupied by a sun disc of the most vivid turquoise, set with pink and red coral rays pointing to the cardinal directions. The sun must be visualized as being suspended in a parallel position above the earth. A spreading tree rises above the sun, filling the upper quarter of the composition with its leafy, flowering branches. A pair of eyes are set just below its spreading branches, and a small human figure is shown reclining within a cartouche perched at the apex of the tree. The Nahuatl word for eye is *ixtli*, and in hieroglyphic writing eyes are used for the value of the root *ix*; *ix*, when used in such phrases as *tlaixco ca*, means "that which is above something," or, as in *ixco*, it may mean "at the summit." It seems reasonable to suppose that the eyes in this composition may have similar meaning, to reinforce the notion that this is a cosmic tree standing above or rising to the summit of the universe. The meaning of the small human figure in the cartouche is not altogether clear, but such figures or faces are frequently shown in combination with celestial cosmic symbols in earlier Mesoamerican art. In addition to their cosmological associations, trees were often metaphorically associated with rulership in sayings that expressed protective qualities:

THOU ART A CYPRESS, THOU ART A SILK COTTON TREE.
BENEATH THEE, / THE COMMON FOLK WILL SEEK THE SHADE; THEY WILL SEEK THE SHADOW.

This saying is said of the rulers who are esteemed like cypresses, like silk cotton trees. Beneath them there is seeking of shade, beneath them there is seeking of shadows. (Sahagún 1951-70, Bk. 6: 252)

Indeed, there were outstanding instances of analogical connection between important tribal offices and the kinds of trees that figure so outstandingly in cosmological accounts. At Tlatelolco, the formerly independent trading city which was annexed by Tenochtitlan, the most important trader's ward was called Pochtlan, "place of the ceiba tree" (from *pochotl*, "ceiba"); traders were themselves called *pochteca*, the most distinguished among them being the *pochtecat-*

zintli. In a figurative sense *pochteca* means mother, father, protector, or governor of a community (Sahagún 1951–70, Bk. 10: 60). This information is presented only to call attention to the fact that symbols describing the structure of the universe, like cult effigies, may also be charged with sociopolitical significance. When the mosaic shield was worn by some great chieftain—perhaps Moctezuma himself—it thus publicly asserted the ruler's link with the governing principle of the universe. Conversely, the cosmogram could be read as an image of the state under the guidance of that chieftain. This suggestion, that *there was among the people of Tenochtitlan a correspondence between the perceptions of state and of cosmos*, is a principal theme that will be explored on the monuments that follow. The last motif on the mosaic shield is the meandering serpent which strikingly unifies the upper and lower registers of the composition. The subject of serpent imagery in Mesoamerican art has yet to be systematically investigated, but it may be speculated that in many instances serpents express a spiritual connection between one entity and another, as between cosmic spheres. Such may be the case in the present instance.

The Dedication Stone: Tenochtitlan as the Center of the World

This famous relief (Fig. 17) was first described by José Fernando Ramírez in an appendix to the first Spanish translation of Prescott's *History of the Conquest of Mexico*, published in Mexico City in 1844–46. Manuel Orozco y Berra later presented a more detailed study of its iconography, and with some modifications his analysis has remained standard until the present time (Orozco y Berra 1877b; Kubler 1962: 57). These studies were primarily addressed to the problem of establishing the specific historical event commemorated on the relief, however, and not to the cosmological frame of reference.

Scholars generally agree that the relief commemorates the completion of the Main Pyramid of Tenochtitlan in the year 1487. The date-glyph 8-Acatl ("reed") corresponding to that year is shown enclosed in the large quadrangular cartouche which occupies more than half the space of the composition. Another *acatl*, with the number seven, appears in the topmost central position of the relief. According to Orozco y Berra, this is *acatl* in its function as a day-sign, corresponding to February 19 (year-signs were ordinarily enclosed in cartouches); Caso's later correlation of the Christian and native calendar systems favors December 18, the time of the annual Panquetzalitztli festivals held in honor of Huitzilopochtli, as the correct reading for this day-sign (Caso 1939). However this may be, it is abundantly clear that the most memorable event of 1487 was the emperor Ahuizotl's dedication of the completed Main Pyramid. At that time Ahuizotl had ruled for barely a year, having been elected to the throne after the premature and somewhat mysterious demise of his brother Tizoc, whose brief rule had not been marked by the military successes required of Mexica emperors. The monarchs confront each other on the upper register of the relief. Both are identified by their respective name-glyphs: Tizoc, "leg of chalk," is on the left, and Ahuizotl, "water dog," or "water monster," is on the right.

The presence of Tizoc is usually explained by asserting that the renovation of the Main Pyramid had been initiated during his reign. But Durán tells us that Moctezuma Ihuilcamina had begun the building operations sometime during the early 1450s and that Tizoc had not notably carried on the work despite the urging of his closest advisor (Durán 1964: 91–2, 180). What seems more plausible as an explanation is that Tizoc is represented here to symbolize the legitimacy of his brother Ahuizotl's accession to power, a power which Ahuizotl magnified and reasserted by carrying to completion the temple begun some thirty years before.

But the commemoration of a specific historical incident and the transferral of power from one monarch to another is only one level of the information transmitted by the Dedication Stone. Its wider significance lies in the identical attire of the emperors, the ritual accessories and ceremonial acts that they perform, and, above all, the setting in which they are depicted. Both

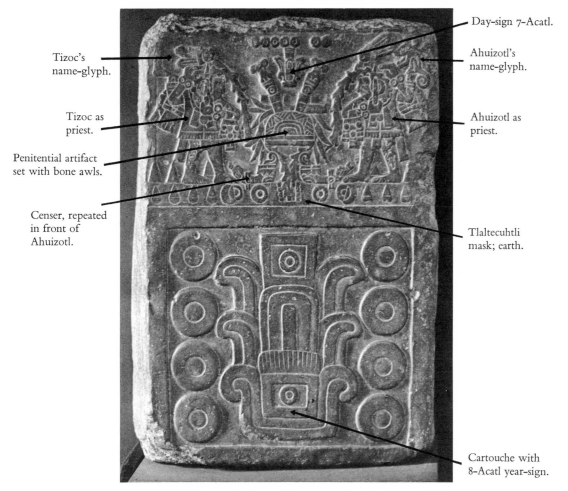

Day-sign 7-Acatl.

Tizoc's
name-glyph.

Ahuizotl's
name-glyph.

Tizoc as
priest.

Ahuizotl as
priest.

Penitential artifact
set with bone awls.

Censer, repeated
in front of
Ahuizotl.

Tlaltecuhtli
mask; earth.

Cartouche with
8-Acatl year-sign.

Fig. 17 The Dedication Stone. Cast in the Museo de la Ciudad de México.

monarchs are clad in the distinctive garments of priests, consisting of shiftlike shirts reaching to the middle of the thigh, bags of copal incense, and back-pouches with elaborate stoppers and folded paper decorations. These pouches were containers for magical potions: mixtures of pitch, ground-up poisonous insects, and tobacco, among other ingredients. Such extraordinary potions were thought to have unusual curative powers when applied to the body, but their principal purpose was to "protect" the wearer when engaged in ritual activities, for all ritual placed the protagonist temporarily in a state of suspension, in an exceptional and therefore dangerous time and place outside the boundaries of normal circumstance. Mexica priests habitually carried these pouches on their lonely nocturnal peregrinations to the shrines of wild forests, caves, and mountain gorges. The last accessories of priestly attire to be depicted here are the long-handled incense-burners which rest upon the ground between the confronting emperors. All these basic garments and accessories are illustrated by a drawing in the Post-Conquest Mendocino Codex (Fig. 18).

Mortification of the flesh was a consistent and recurring practice in almost all Mexica religious events.

Fig. 18 At the left stands a priestly figure with *xicolli* shirt, censer, incense bag, and container on his back. In the center, a figure drums below the stars (represented by eyes). Codex Mendocino, p. 63.

Maguey-cactus thorns (see Fig. 2), bone awls, and obsidian blades were used to draw blood from various parts of the body in penitential rites. The theme of penitence and sacrifice is clearly represented by the central motif of the composition, a woven grass hemisphere set with ornamented awls. An arrangement of precious feathers completes this artifact. Tizoc and Ahuizotl both display wounds on their legs, and both perforate their ears with exaggerated bone awls. Two thick streams of blood flow from their ears down into the open jaws of Tlaltecuhtli, represented here by another abbreviated mask displaying the familiar tooth-studded open jaws, a pair of circular jade pieces, and two lidded eyes on either side. Other references to the earth are made by drop-shaped elements representing reptilian scales, and by triangular shapes which rest upon the ground-line. The latter probably allude to the serrated back of *cipactli*, the earth-alligator.

The emperors are depicted here in their traditional role as the chief spiritual stewards of the nation. No definitive study of the Mexica priesthood has yet appeared in the anthropological literature (Miguel Acosta Saignes [1946] has made the most comprehensive study to date), but it does seem likely that in earliest Mexica tradition the tribal leader had combined the offices of secular chieftain and head of the religious establishment. This is of course suggested by the historical accounts describing Huitzilopochtli. The pattern of identifying community leaders with the forces of nature has already been discussed. Even though religious and secular offices were distinctly defined by the middle of the fifteenth century, due to the complexities of administering an empire, the supreme monarch continued to act symbolically as the primate of the priestly hierarchy. His role as the spiritual leader of the nation was emphasized in every coronation ceremony, as is illustrated by Nezahualpilli's discourse to Moctezuma Xocoyotzin when the latter was elected ruler of Tenochtitlan in 1502:

". . . Because of the cares of the kingdom you must be wakeful. You must rise early and go out to watch the stars in order to observe their movements, signs, influences and omens. You must be ready to receive the morning star and, as soon as it appears, you must take your ritual bath, purifying yourself and anointing yourself with the divine pitch. You will then bleed yourself and, carrying the incense burner, you will offer incense and sacrifice to the gods. Finally, you will contemplate the hidden places and the nine folds of the heavens. You will descend to the place of the abyss, to the center of the earth, where stand the three houses of fire. You will go to the hills and wilderness where the sons of God do penance and live in the solitude of caves, and you will also contemplate the divine springs and streams.

"You must care for and remember all these things, especially those connected with the divine cult and reverence of the gods and honor the priesthood. You must see that the latter continue their penance and you must give them courage and aid. With these words I end my discourse." (Durán 1964: 222)

The dedication of new temples is specifically mentioned as an occasion in which the ruler appeared attired in priestly garments. In describing the ceremonies involved in dedicating the *coateocalli*, the "serpent-temple" where idols from all the different provinces and lands were kept, Durán recounts the following sequence of events:

When the victorious army returned to Mexico Moteczoma dressed himself in the garments of the high priest, anointed his body with the divine bitumen and took a golden incense burner in his hands. He then entered the place where all the idols had been gathered, brought from all the nations and representing all created things. Having incensed them and having performed all the ceremonies that were usual when a temple or a house was to be used for the first time, he and Cihuacoatl came to the place of sacrifice which stood outside of the doorway to the shrine. The prisoners who had been brought from Teuctepec were then sacrificed. (Durán 1964: 237)

The dates, the event, the personages, the ceremonies and institutions portrayed on the Dedication Stone were historic realities of fifteenth-century Tenochtitlan. Nothing is mythological, a fact that will be important to bear in mind when interpreting other monuments of a commemorative nature. In this context, Tlaltecuhtli-cipactli takes on a dual meaning: it is not only a symbol of the sacred earth, it is the earth of Tenochtitlan itself: *cem anahuac tenochca tlalpan*, "the world, Tenochca (Mexica) land." The sacred earth is here a metaphor for the territory of the nation. The open jaws of Tlaltecuhtli provide symbolic access to the "heart of the earth," the conceptual place of the earth's procreative and sustaining force, the *omphalos* of the universe; correspondingly, the main ceremonial center of Tenochtitlan acted not only as the central point of reference for the city, but also for the empire. The city, and by extension the empire, was conceived and modeled in terms of cosmological structure, and through this identification the nation automatically asserted its sacred identity and centrality in the Mesoamerican world.

The Stone of Tizoc: Expansion of the Mexica Cosmos

As foreign nations fell by force of arms or were otherwise coerced into becoming tributaries of Tenochtitlan, they became symbolically incorporated into the world of which that city was the center. Large-scale sculptural monuments were commissioned to advertise this process with depictions of cosmological settings within which foreign nations expressed their submission in terms of ritual acts.

Manuel Orozco y Berra recounts the story of the discovery of the Stone of Tizoc (Figs. 19, 20). It was unearthed in 1791 by workmen engaged in repaving the main plaza of downtown Mexico City. Apparently, there had been a number of other monuments found during this project, all of which were broken up on the spot to be used for cobblestones. Fortunately, in this instance, a priest named Gamboa happened to be walking by, saw the sculpture, and prevented its destruction by having it removed to the nearby cathedral atrium. The monument remained there until 1824, when it was transferred to the patio of the old university (Orozco y Berra 1877a: 16), where it remained until its recent removal to the Mexica Hall of the new Museum of Anthropology. It is said that other monuments like the Stone of Tizoc remain buried in the debris of Tenochtitlan beneath the plaza surface, but no attempt has yet been made to excavate the area systematically. It is surely reasonable to assume that this sculpture was one of a related series, for it validates the rule of Tizoc; other emperors may well have commissioned similar monuments to perpetuate the memory of their reign.

Tizoc, the seventh monarch of Tenochtitlan, is identified by his name-glyph at the beginning of a sequence of fifteen nearly identical scenes. In this initial

Fig..19 (left) The Stone of Tizoc. Photo courtesy of the Museo Nacional de Antropología, Mexico.

Fig. 20 (below) The Stone of Tizoc (after Orozco y Berra 1877a).

scene he is shown wearing an elaborate plumed head-dress with a bird's beak framing his face: Orozco y Berra's drawing of this beak is indistinct, but it may be the hummingbird headdress characteristic of Huit-zilopochtli (a similar headdress is clearly depicted on a figure of Huitzilopochtli on the Teocalli of Sacred Warfare Stone, which will be examined shortly). Ti-zoc is also qualified by a "smoking-foot" motif, com-monly associated with Tezcatlipoca; but in a general metaphoric sense, smoke or mist could also refer sim-ply to command, fame, or honor. The emperor faces a foreign chieftain, identified by the distinctive head-dress of his nation and by the place-glyph of his city; this chieftain inclines forward slightly as Tizoc grasps him by the scalplock. It is commonly assumed that this is a symbolic "capture" alluding to military con-quest. This basic arrangement is repeated by the re-maining figures of the relief, though the place-glyphs and the attire of the foreign chieftains is different in every instance; also, Tizoc is identified by name only in the initial scene, and he alone is depicted with a par-ticularly large headdress; the remaining "capturing" figures all wear identical smaller headdresses, yet all are shown with the "smoking foot." These capturing figures may thus be taken to represent Mexica cap-tains or allied military chieftains. It has been rightly observed that many if not all of the places identified in this sequence were conquered by earlier emperors, and that Tizoc is, therefore, shown as a symbolic con-queror, the inheritor of empire.

This traditional interpretation may be modified by noting that all important state events were invariably marked by the sacrifice of prisoners actually captured by Mexica armies in the field, or of prisoners given over by tributary nations in token of submission to Tenochtitlan. For instance, the dedication of the Main Pyramid was marked by an exceptional number of immolations; it is recounted that sacrificial prisoners from many places were lined up from the ceremonial center all the way out onto the causeways. Military tri-umphs, coronations, and imperial funerals were simi-larly celebrated. The "capture" scenes may, therefore, not allude directly to the military conquests of earlier emperors, but rather to the symbolic contribution of sacrificial victims by subject cities, as a ritual act of obeisance to Tenochtitlan at the time of Tizoc's ac-cession to the throne. Thus Tizoc and other unnamed Mexica lords appear to be symbolically acknowledg-ing such transactions.

All these figures are depicted in a cosmological set-ting. The earth is represented below by a strip set with four abbreviated Tlaltecuhtli masks placed at the car-dinal points. The earth has its counterpart above in a celestial band, represented by eyes and circular pieces of jade symbolizing stars and precious quality, re-spectively. The entire top of the cylindrical cosmo-gram is carved with a complex sun diadem, equipped with four large rays pointing in the direction of the cardinal points in correspondence with the position of the Tlaltecuhtli masks below. The intercardinal points are indicated by the smaller intermediate rays. While the "capture" scenes were traditionally recognized in terms of conquest, and the sun diadem was also iden-tified in nineteenth-century descriptions of the mon-ument, the earth and sky bands were not recognized at first (Orozco y Berra 1877a). Consequently, most scholars attempted to establish the stone either as a *temalacatl*—a circular stone of gladiatorial combat— or as a kind of elaborate *cuauhxicalli*—a sacrificial re-ceptacle for human hearts. The *cuauhxicalli* argument arose in response to the puzzling hollowed-out center of the sun diadem, with its groove running out to the edge. This hollow is demonstrably a mutilation, how-ever, probably carried out in early Colonial times for unknown purposes. It cannot have formed part of the original composition, for it is not only crudely exe-cuted, but the channel also arbitrarily cuts across the symmetrical solar design. *Temalacatl* stones have a bar carved into the center, to which enemy champions were tied for ritual combat with Mexica warriors. We cannot altogether discard the possibility that a bar did once exist across the hollow cup in the center of the Tizoc Stone, but even this should not obscure the primary meaning and function of the monument. In recent years a suggestive comment concerning the cos-mological significance of the composition was made by Kubler, who remarked that Tizoc is depicted as the inheritor of many conquests, "the lord of all between earth and heaven" (Kubler 1962: 57).

Unlike such famous monuments of Roman antiquity as the columns of Trajan and Marcus Aurelius, which present a continuous narrative of the emperor's campaigns in all the emotion, detail, and incident of daily life, the Stone of Tizoc defines empire in terms of acts of ritual submission unfolding in a stark cosmological setting. The ritualistic aspect of the monument is underlined by the fact that the fifteen scenes are depicted in a counterclockwise sequence determined by the position of Tizoc. The emperor faces right, as do his Mexica chiefs, all of whom describe a circuit corresponding to, and determined by, the idealized perimeter of the universe. The ritual incorporation of subject peoples into an imperium thus symbolically conforms to cosmic structure. It is worth pausing to reinforce this point with some additional observations concerning ceremonial circuits as they were performed in the public processions and dances of Tenochtitlan. In their most spectacular form these processions took place around the perimeter of the ritual concourse of the main ceremonial center on occasions of particular importance. Sahagún writes of one such procession as it was held every four years during the *Izcalli* festivals, which took place just before the onset of the dreaded unnamed and uncounted days of *nemontemi*, the time of suspended animation before the advent of the new year and the rebirth of life:

And when they had completely ended the slaying, when it was so, [then] all the chiefs and lords, who were men due great reverence, were ready, and stood waiting in complete array. Moctezuma led them. He had put on the turquoise diadem, the royal diadem.

. . . .

And in their hands were staves, which were small and shaped like weaving sticks and painted in two colors—red above and chalky white below. In either hand they grasped a paper incense bag. Thereupon they came down [from the temple], dancing rapidly.

And when they had descended, then they circled [the courtyard] . . . only four times. And when they had danced, then they dispersed and went away, and thereupon all en-

tered the palace in proper order. And this was known as the Lordly Dance; . . . it was the privilege exclusively of the chiefs that they should dance the Lordly Dance. (Sahagún 1951–70, Bk. 2: 151–2)

The main ceremonial precinct of Tenochtitlan, which was the site of this Lordly Dance, had, among many other buildings, a series of small shrines set around the edge of the principal ritual concourse. These shrines belonged to the four main wards of the city. In addition to these ward shrines, the enclosure featured a tree-lined processional roadway around its inner perimeter. This ensemble was at once the most crucial social space in the empire, as well as the most sanctified: it was, in effect, a microcosm of the city and a microcosm of the universe. In the Lordly Dance we find Moctezuma and all the magnates of the nation describing four circuits around this cardinally oriented quadrangle. After facing this space from the east-west axis determined by the principal pyramid and the path of the sun, they move around the concourse to purify the nation symbolically before the onset of *nemontemi*, reaffirming the interrelationship of the social and the cosmic orders. The primary conceptual model for the function of the emperor and for the circumambulation of the dance is expressed by the term *Ipalnemoani*: "lord of the near, and of that contained within the circuit."

Sahagún does not specify counterclockwise movement, but we may infer from other sources that it was the prescribed direction of this and related dances and processions. Durán (1963: Trat. 2, Lám. 11) illustrates the matter in his *Atlas* (Fig. 21), and counterclockwise processions persisted in a Christian context throughout the sixteenth century, due to an extraordinary convergence and compatibility of Indian and Spanish practices. The immense popularity of the large colonial mission atriums with their processional ways, their four *posa* chapels at the intercardinal points, and the relationship of the whole east-west axis of the church itself, is directly attributable to the significance that cosmological models held in the Indian tradition (MacAndrew 1965; Kubler 1948). Atriums enjoyed great popularity in Early Christian times and during

Fig. 21 Counterclockwise movement of the dance (after Durán 1963: Trat. 2, Lám. 11).

the first golden age of Byzantium, but had largely fallen into disuse well before the sixteenth century. Their revival and elaboration in the sixteenth-century missions of New Spain responded to Indian receptivity, and although the most perceptive friars were doubtlessly aware that heathen custom persisted in these new architectural contexts, the policy for Christian conversion called for patience and adaptability as well as a firm hand in dealing with ancient practices (for a description of ceremonial circuits as practiced in a contemporary Maya Indian community in Chiapas, Mexico, see Vogt 1969).

The Stone of Tizoc illustrates how the structure of the universe was conceived as the model for social space at Tenochtitlan. Social space was automatically translated as sacred space, to be separated and purified against the inchoate, threatening forces and phenomena of regions barely known, of foreign territories beyond the zone of Mexican habitation and control. The circuits defining the boundaries of social space replicated the geometric structure that the universe

was thought to have: it was as if the air within these boundaries was charged with a palpably different frequency that heightened the identity of the nation, the city, the ward, the clan, and the individual. It is necessary to remind ourselves that "cosmos," in that time and place, did not have the vast dimensions that it has for us today. As a matter of course, this model was magnified and projected to include the tributary nations of the Mexica state. It could not have been otherwise. Conquered nations throughout the empire expressed continuing submission to the new emperor and his lords, and thereby became ritually incorporated into the Mexica world. That this world was conceived as cosmos is spelled out by the arrangement of cosmic symbols on this circular monument, and by the symbolic circumambulation of the Mexica chieftains. In their ambition to become the conquerors and heirs of an ancient civilization, and in their interpretation of that ambition as a sacred mission, the Mexica fused metaphysics and ordinary human vanity; but considering even the rapacious motives of the state, their vision of a sacred imperial cosmos held the promise, if only on Mexica terms, of a much less fragmented Mesoamerica.

The Teocalli of Sacred War: Symbolic Regeneration of the Empire

The miniature *teocalli*, or temple (Fig. 22), was originally discovered embedded in the foundations of the National Palace of Mexico City in 1831, but almost a full century elapsed until it was finally removed during alterations to the building in 1926. Within months of the rediscovery, Alfonso Caso published a theory that the images of gods, cosmic symbols, ritual artifacts, and date-glyphs which cover the surfaces of the monument refer to the myth of sacrificial genesis, a myth that justified human sacrifice and warranted warfare as a means of procuring prisoners for immolation in the temples of Tenochtitlan (Caso 1927). Caso regarded this myth as the foundation of a mystical-military ideology whereby the Mexica conceived themselves to be the chosen people of the sun, responsible for ensuring the continuity of the universe through human sacrifice. The Teocalli was thus interpreted as an illustrative allegory comparable to such Hellenistic sculpture as the Altar of Zeus at Pergamon, which represents a mythological theme as an allusive paradigm for contemporary historical events and political philosophy.

Another analysis of the monument by Enrique Juan Palacios (1929) also appeared soon after the monument was brought to light. Palacios explores similar possibilities of interpretation, but he also brought out aspects of the iconography that could be interpreted in a more directly historical, less allegorical fashion. Some of these observations are especially pertinent in the perspective afforded by the other monuments we have seen, which stress abstract cosmological settings populated by identifiably historical personages, but not by gods. These settings are not the landscapes of mythology, but cosmograms representing the sacred nature of the Mexica nation and all that fell beneath its rule.

Caso's views received particularly widespread recognition, for they were later incorporated into his influential writings on the subject of Mexica religion. It was his notion that the prime motivation and impetus of Mexica civilization came from religion, above all from a sense of collaboration with the gods in maintaining the order of the cosmos through compulsive sacrifice (Caso 1936, 1958; see also Kubler 1962: 51–63). These views were naturally greatly conditioned by traditionally accepted ideas concerning a pantheon of gods, and also by an assumption that the immutable activities of gods, as portrayed in myths, were unalterable models for shaping cultural behavior at Tenochtitlan.

It is quite unlikely that the Mexica were somehow compelled to an unquestioning repetition of mythological archetypes, for myths could be adapted, regenerated, or created anew according to the policies of imperial states. While a sense of divine mission surely lent impetus and inspiration to conquest, such convictions must also have been visualized and forcefully promoted by powerful rulers wishing to unite a nation in imperial endeavors. Examples of this pattern abound in Old World history as well as in the Americas: in the fourth century A.D., the emperor Constantine convoked the Council of Nicea as the culmination of a series of councils aimed at canonizing a previously more fluid theological situation to suit conditions already partly determined by political realities; similarly, the emperor Pachacuti had reorganized the Inca religious system during the fifteenth century as a step to secure an integrated ideological structure for a vast Andean empire.

Mesoamerican phenomena must be explained by more than simple analogies with other civilizations, however, and since Caso's interpretation of the Teocalli is so well known and is so intimately bound up with his widely accepted notions of the role of religion in Mexica culture, we shall pause to review briefly this key myth of sacrificial genesis. In doing so, we are necessarily obliged to reinterpret the myth in the light of what has already been established concerning the metaphoric language used to express the mag-

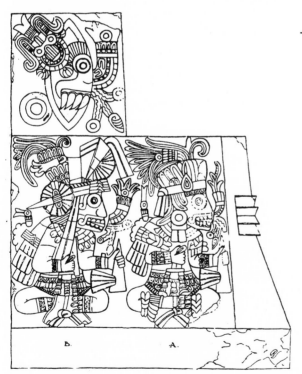

Fig. 22a. (far left, above) The Teocalli of Sacred Warfare. Photo courtesy of the Museo Nacional de Antropología, Mexico. b. (left, above) Front of the Teocalli. c. (above) Top view, looking towards the front: above, the stairs, Tlaltecuhtli, and flanking shields; below, a penitential artifact, a 2-Calli date, and flanking *xiuhcoatl* torches. d. (right, above) Rear view: above, the eagle and cactus; below, sketched-in *tetl* element (an abbreviated Tlaltecuhtli mask; see Figure 23a) resting upon the belly of Chalchihuitlicue. e. (left, below) Left side. f. (right, below) Right side. (Line drawings b–f after Palacios 1929: Figs. 1, 5, 2, 3, 4.)

C.   D.

ical and hallowed nature of the natural forces; it will also be useful to comment on the reasons why the sacrificial aspects of genesis stories came to be so important in the process of creating an imperial ideology at Tenochtitlan.

Genesis accounts vary in detail among the various peoples of the Central Highlands; it is nevertheless possible to identify a fundamental sequence of events leading to the sacrificial episodes that were so important in the Mexica ideological system (Nicholson 1973). The most complete accounts open with a description of the primordial male-female source of life (Ometecuhtli, Omecihuatl, etc.). This is usually followed by metaphoric passages describing the birth of such prominent tribal avatars and heroes as Huitzilopochtli, Tezcatlipoca, Mixcoatl, Quetzalcoatl, and so forth; this should not be taken in a literal sense as the birth of gods, but as a figurative way of establishing the authenticity and divinity of these ancestral personages by expressing their connection with the generative nucleus of the universe. Some sources similarly establish the cosmological associations of these personages through metaphoric images that place them in the four quarters of the universe at once: thus, there was said to be a Tezcatlipoca of the north, of the south, of the east, and of the west; such images of magical elasticity were also admirably suited to express the political influence of a given nation in cosmological terms. The identification of tribal patrons with creative and civilizing activities was also expressed by attributing to them the creation of fire, of the heavens and the earth, of rain and water, and of the first human couple. In sum, each nation sought to legitimize itself by affirming the connection of their respective tribal patrons with the time and space of genesis. On a more abstract level, these stories also expressed the sacred nature of the elements by virtue of their ultimate derivation from the universal life-source.

The opening events of genesis were followed by a succession of four eras, called "suns," a notion not unlike the concept of *kalpas* in Hindu mythology. Each sun was thought to have lasted a specific number of years, and each had a determined set of characteristics terminating in cataclysmic destruction before the end of the fifth, or present, sun. This fifth era began when the date 1-Tochtli (1-Rabbit, A.D. 882) closed out the old cycle, and 2-Acatl (2-Reed, A.D. 883) ushered in the new. This new era was called Ollintonatiuh, "movement sun," or "earthquake sun." (The present era was predicted to end in earthquakes.) According to some accounts, it fell to Quetzalcoatl and Tezcatlipoca, the two paramount cult figures of Postclassic times before the advent of Huitzilopochtli, to initiate the reconstruction of the world and civilization after the collapse of the fourth era. Their creative role was symbolized in mythological tales recounting their magical transformation into cosmic trees which raised the fallen sky with the help of the four sky-bearers that were especially created to support the heavens at the intercardinal points. In one story, both heroes enter the body of Tlaltecuhtli to meet at the heart, or center, to raise the celestial sphere. In short, the semilegendary historic leaders of Mesoamerican antiquity were metaphorically linked with cosmological processes and were thus magnified as sacred characters.

One story tells that the sun and the moon, fire, man's sustenance, and present mankind were created at the beginning of the present era when Quetzalcoatl descended to the world of the dead to gather the bones of past generations, which he retrieved to take back to Tamoanchan (probably another name for Omeyocan, "place of duality"). These bones are then ground up and made into dough with the help of Quetzalcoatl's own blood, and from this consecrated mixture mankind is fashioned. León-Portilla has rightly observed that in this tale Quetzalcoatl and Cihuacoatl —"serpent woman," who had done the actual mixing —are equated with Ometecuhtli and Omecihuatl, the primordial male-female creative principle. Following this, Quetzalcoatl made an unsuccessful attempt to acquire maize, amaranth, chia, and other food staples cultivated by the Highlands peoples. This attempt was finally carried out by Nanahuatl (sometimes spelled Nanahuatzin, "respected one afflicted with tumors"; the ethnic affiliation of this obscure personage is unclear). Afterwards, Nanahuatzin created the sun by jumping into a great bonfire to emerge later as the sun itself. This auto-sacrifice was immediately followed by another, when Tecuciztecatl, "conch-shell lord," also immolated himself to become the moon. (Tecuciztecatl was the focus of a major cult at Xaltocan, the ancient island-capital of the Otomí nation, located in the lake to the north of Lake Texcoco.) The sun and moon were still stationary at this point, and were only set in motion when Quetzalcoatl slew an "assembly of gods" and then summoned Ehecatl, the wind, to propel the celestial bodies across the sky. One tale has it that the "assembly of gods" sacrificed themselves of their own accord. Again we must remind ourselves that the multiplicity of metaphoric names corresponds not only to the diversity of natural phenomena and their respective cults, but also to the diversity of peoples within the Highlands and the names of their respective ancestral heroes, identified with those cults.

Caso held that the sacrifices involved in the creation of the present era established an archetypal blood-debt, conferring upon mankind the responsibility to continue sacrifice as an exchange of vitality that would ensure the perpetuation of the universe. For this reason, war was instituted to obtain prisoners; war became a sacred obligation. It has been observed that these beliefs and practices must be of ancient origin, for scenes of sacrifice figure outstandingly in the arts of earlier Mesoamerican peoples, particularly in the Postclassic Toltec period. The *Anales de Cuauhtitlan* specifically remark on the expanded role of human sacrifice under the reign of Huemac at Tula (A.D. 995 to 1018), another fact suggesting that there may be some historical basis to the myths in question (*Anales de Cuauhtitlan* in *Codice Chimalpopocatl*, comp. José Fernando Ramírez 1885).

In any event, it is abundantly clear that the Mexica seized upon these beliefs and practices, accentuating human sacrifice beyond all earlier measure. But was the Mexica nation actually held in thrall to this myth of blood-debt, as is so often asserted, or were sacrificial practices singled out and purposely magnified as part of a program of imperial policy? The mass im-

molation of prisoners of war was not common practice among the other warlike peoples of the Highlands prior to the rise of Tenochtitlan, and such practices were resisted at Texcoco even after the Mexica alliance. Faith in the myth of sacrificial creation undoubtedly contributed in creating a sense of divine mission, but to assume that men of such tough, ruthless, and ambitious character as Itzcoatl, Tlacaelel, Moctezuma Ihuilcamina, and Ahuizotl were in some way held in bondage to a myth of blood-debt is to ignore their own capacity for mythmaking, or for emphasizing aspects of a traditional mythology to justify rapacious policies, to inure the population to violence, and to strike terror among the enemies of the nation. The political aspect of mass sacrifices is well illustrated by Durán (1964: 190–9) in his descriptions of the ceremonies held by Tlacaelel and Ahuizotl during the dedication of the Main Pyramid of Tenochtitlan. The event was highly publicized throughout the land and was attended not only by the Mexica and their allies, but also by the chieftains and magnates of many hostile regions. These enemy potentates had been granted special safe-passes and were carefully hidden from public view during their stay at Tenochtitlan:

> Later the captives that had been brought for the sacrifice were formed in a line. . . . They were men from Huexotzinco, Tlaxcala, Atlixco, Tiliuhquitepec, Cholula, Tecoac, Zacatlan. . . . King Ahuizotl was greatly satisfied and he sat upon the royal throne, showing his grandeur to all the nations, the magnificence of his empire and the courage of his people. The two allied monarchs from Texcoco and Tacuba sat next to him, and the enemy rulers were seated in a place where they could see without being seen.
>
> Ahuizotl then ordered the royal officials to have the stewards, administrators, and treasurers of all the provinces bring in the royal tribute. . . . The first tribute bearers were those of the city of Mexico, then those of Xochimilco and its neighbors, Chalco, of Coixtlahuaca in the land of the Mixtecs, of Tochpan. . . .
>
> All of these men brought offerings so great in value and quantity that the enemies, guests, and strangers were bewildered, amazed. They saw the Aztecs were masters of the entire world and they realized that the Aztec people had conquered all the nations and that all were their vassals. (Durán 1964: 194–5)

Durán (1964: 199) concludes his lengthy description by telling of four full days of sacrifices that followed the opening ceremonies, sacrifices in which Ahuizotl and his closest advisors directly participated to set a personal example. The foreign ambassadors and guests then departed, "bewildered by the majesty of the city and the amazing number of victims who had died."

Obsessive religious compulsion was clearly not the only major impulse of Mexica life, nor was it the sole impelling force driving them to the conquest of Meso-america. Religion was simply the language, the vehicle, for a spectrum of ambitions and endeavors that were authenticated by a sense of participation in the transcendent reality of the cosmos. The accentuation of human sacrifice was only part of a major program of ideological reformulation in progress at Tenochtitlan. The rulers of Tenochtitlan had not only commissioned the rewriting of history to reflect their national identity in a more favorable light, but they had also initiated the reorganization of ceremonial practices and a corresponding readjustment of mythology to reflect an imperial policy and mystique. The Nahuatl texts describing ceremonial procedures with mythological explanations reveal a tendency to join myths from a diversity of festivals held for a wide variety of purposes. Many instances occur in which one ritual is substituted for another, and in which various mythological explanations are given for a single ritual (Hvidtfeldt 1958). This inconsistency may be partly attributed to the confusions and spontaneous associations that occur on a popular level in any new and heterogeneous urban society; but the general pattern strongly indicates that state policy played an important role in coordinating a variety of similar regional cults to express a more coherent state religious ideology. Coordination and integration of the religious life held the promise of consensus about the values which should guide social behavior throughout the far-flung dominions. Despite its unprecedentedly barbarous tenor, ceremonial life at Tenochtitlan must be recognized as an imaginative effort to create an integrated ideology for Mesoamerica. For these reasons purely mythological interpretations of the Teocalli must be questioned, without altogether discarding the probability of mythological content. It is a matter of assessing the information presented by the figures of this monument in the wider context of the actual time, place, and circumstance of Tenochtitlan.

The Teocalli reproduces standard forms of Late Postclassic temple architecture. Characteristically, the stairway is flanked by sloping balustrades which change to a vertical pitch as they approach the temple platform. The sanctuary itself is represented by a block displaying an elaborate sun-disc in the position corresponding to the altarpiece. Since temples were symbolic of community identity we may surmise that the model temple was an ideogram of the Mexica nation. The thirteen steps of the staircase may perhaps have some esoteric significance in connection with the thirteen heavenly planes, but on a more general level of meaning they probably signify magnitude of sacred power. Both these balustrades bear date-glyphs below: 1-Tochtli ("rabbit"), to the left, and 2-Acatl ("reed"), to the right. We may recall that these dates are those of the beginning of the present era, and it was Caso's (1927: 62–3) view that they indeed did refer to that mythological time. But these are the dates that also mark the opening and closing of *any* 52-year cycle in the native calendar; with this in mind, Palacios (1929: 20–1) called attention to the possibility that they might refer to the cycle that began in 1507. The New Fire ceremonies held atop Huixtocihuatl (the Cerro de la Estrella, between Lake Texcoco and Lake Xochimilco) were important events in 1507, and are reported in some detail by the sixteenth-century chroniclers. A pair of ritual vessels complete the balustrade ensemble near the top: these are without question *cuauhxicallis*, ceremonial containers for sacrificial hearts. The eagle feathers and jaguar spots with which they are respectively adorned are emblematic of the Mexica warrior orders.

Ascending the stairway we abruptly encounter the open jaws of Tlaltecuhtli, carved in relief upon the sanctuary platform floor (Fig. 22c). This figure is depicted in full ritual attire with clawed extremities, the braided pendant apron, and the stylized skull at the small of the back. Tlaltecuhtli is flanked by a pair of shields with flags and bundles of arrows. Palacios and Caso both interpreted these figures in terms of their relationship to the altarpiece relief, and we shall follow suit for the sake of putting their argument into an historical, as opposed to a purely mythological, context.

The central element of the altarpiece is an elaborate sun-disc with the 4-Ollin ("movement") glyph (Fig. 22b). This is unmistakably the sign of the present era, Ollintonatiuh; it also stands for the actual, physical sun. The sun was not only worshiped as a source of heat and life, but it was metaphorically regarded as a symbol of the era of Mexica rule and its cult was the special responsibility of the Mexica warrior orders, just as other professions were responsible for the cults of vegetation, water, or rain. The sun-cult naturally had a special significance for the nation since the warrior aristocracy occupied such a paramount position in the social and economic hierarchy of Tenochtitlan. This significance is underlined by the flanking figures of Huitzilopochtli (left) and Tezcatlipoca (right). The impersonator of Huitzilopochtli wears a hummingbird headdress and another emblematic item, a footcovering in the form of *xiuhcoatl*, "turquoise serpent," commonly associated with fire and solar heat. The date-glyph 1-Tecpatl ("stone knife") is carved upon the outside sanctuary panel next to Huitzilopochtli (Fig. 22e): according to some accounts it is the date on which the Mexica initiated their historic migration to the Valley of Mexico; it is also a date calendrically associated with Huitzilopochtli's influence. The identification of Tezcatlipoca is somewhat less clear and depends in part on circumstantial evidence. Many sources describe him as Huitzilopochtli's "brother," and we have already read Bernal Díaz's eyewitness report of their images placed side by side at the Tlatelolco temple. The cult was preeminently centered at Texcoco, where it was naturally associated with the royal house, a fact that appears to be alluded to by the small royal diadem seen above and just in front of Tezcatlipoca's figure on the Teocalli. The jaguar was an animal frequently linked to Tezcatlipoca, and a

jaguar headdress is here shown on the impersonator's back. Finally, the date 1-Miquiztli ("death") seen on the right outside panel of the sanctuary is notably connected with Tezcatlipoca's influence (Fig. 22f). Like the confronted figures of Tizoc and Ahuizotl on the Dedication Stone, the confronted impersonators of Huitzilopochtli and Tezcatlipoca carry bags of copal and maguey cactus leaves set with penitential spines. Both utter the speech-glyph *atl-tlachinolli*, meaning war; this war-cry is repeated by the faces of the 1-Tecpatl and 1-Miquiztli date-glyphs on the side panels.

We shall now return to the reliefs of the platform floor to discuss their relationship with the "altarpiece" just examined. Certain cosmological stories describe the setting sun as being "eaten" by the earth, and both Caso and Palacios thought that the "reversed" position of Tlaltecuhtli in relation to the sun-disc meant that the latter was to be considered the "renascent" sun of the morning, a symbol of triumph for the Mexica, the sun's chosen people. But the position of Tlaltecuhtli is actually more directly related to the stairway. Were we to ascend the stairway in our imagination, we would find ourselves entering the open jaws to stand within, or upon, the body of the earth. Tlaltecuhtli is here once again *cem anahuac tenochca tlalpan*, "the world, Tenochca (Mexica) land." This is confirmed by the shields and arrows, which indicate the appropriation of territory by force of arms. There can be no doubt about this meaning, for shields and arrows were standard images of conquest in prophetic recitations. The *Crónica Mexicayotl* recounts the following speech, said to have been made by Huitzilopochtli himself through the medium of his idol-bearers:

> When I came forth, when I was sent here,
> I was given arrows and a shield,
> for battle is my work.
> And with my belly, with my head,
> I shall confront cities everywhere.
> I shall await the peoples from the four directions,
> I shall join battle with them,
> I shall provide people with drink,
> I shall provide them with food!
> Here I shall bring together the diverse peoples,

and not in vain, for I shall conquer them,
  that I may see the house of jade, the house of gold,
    the house of quetzal feathers;
  the house of emeralds, the house of coral,
    the house of amethysts;
  and sundry feathers—the lovely cotinga feathers,
    the roseate spoonbill feathers, the trogon feathers—
  all the precious feathers;
  and the *cacao* of variegated colors!
        (Alvarado Tezozomoc 1971: 316)

In this prophetic announcement, which took place at Coatepec during the Mexica wanderings, the tribal avatar visualizes security and success for his nation in terms of conquest and the acquisition of treasures. The "houses" are perhaps palace treasure rooms, such as the one so vividly described by Bernal Díaz in the Palace of Moctezuma, secretly opened and later plundered by the Spanish at the time of the desperate flight from Tenochtitlan on the Noche Triste. Warfare was automatically hallowed by the command of a sacred tribal oracle, and in the motivation for imperial expansion, the metaphysical and material were automatically fused into a calling.

The hieratic composition of the altarpiece and the reliefs upon the platform floor in front of it reveal how the Mexica portrayed themselves as the rulers of the earth in the present era. Huitzilopochtli, the national patron of the Mexica overlords, is shown to be on an equal footing with the ancient and more prestigious Tezcatlipoca, whose cult was so intimately tied to the royal house of Texcoco. To be sure, the political and military alliance of the two capitals is acknowledged here; but already Tezcatlipoca begins to act in a new, almost exclusively Mexica capacity; his cult is, so to speak, appropriated and absorbed by the newcomers in their growing sense of belonging to the association of the greatest ruling nations of Mesoamerica. The primary function of Tezcatlipoca on this monument is to proclaim a legitimacy of succession in which the Mexica nation would become the authentic heirs to the Mesoamerican world.

The famous relief carved upon the rear of the Teocalli depicts the place-glyph of Tenochtitlan surmounted by an eagle (Fig. 22d). Surely the Texcocan glyph would have been included had it been the purpose of this monument to celebrate the partnership of nations. The place-glyph for Tenochtitlan (*tetl*, "rock," *nochtli*, "fruit of the nopal cactus," *tlan*, "at," "upon," etc.) is that of a fruit-laden nopal cactus springing from a rock. Curiously, Caso (1927: 54–61) did not identify the requisite *tetl* component because of the mutilation of the lower portion of the relief. This omission substantially changed the meaning of the relief in his report. But, as is often the case in deciphering the eroded or defaced monuments of Mesoamerica, the traces of original lines may escape one investigator, to be revealed at another time, sometimes due to different lighting conditions. Seen in sharply raking light, the *tetl* element stands out as an abbreviated, oval-shaped Tlaltecuhtli-mask separated from the torso of a larger recumbent figure by the clear trace of a semicircular line running from eye to eye down below the bottom of the mouth (Fig. 23a).

The recumbent figure is Chalchihuitlicue, "she of the jade skirts." Although the headdress and torso are almost completely effaced, the lower legs and feet are clearly represented to the right, emerging from a skirt ornamented with wavy lines and circular jade-pieces (the knees are drawn up behind an intervening cactus-fruit). The pattern of the skirt is echoed by the watery background. We are unmistakably given to understand that this is a lake, Lake Texcoco.

The place-glyph of Tenochtitlan with the eagle devouring a cactus fruit is more than a hieroglyphic, linguistic image, for it also represents a magical vision said to have been witnessed by the Mexican magnates on the spot that was to become their capital. It is hardly necessary to recount this legend in detail, for it is probably the most familiar of all in Mesoamerican literature. It will be remembered that the Mexica had originally been forced to flee to their marshy refuge in Lake Texcoco after a disastrous altercation with the Lord of Culhuacan, sometime around 1325. At some undetermined later time these unseemly and humiliating circumstances were minimized; the founding of the city was given dignity by representing it as the fulfillment of a prophetic announcement by Huitzilo-

Fig. 23*a*. (left) Sketch of rear of the Teocalli, showing trace of the *tetl* element (an abbreviated Tlaltecuhtli mask) in relation to the recumbent Chalchihuitlicue. *b*. (above) A similar image from the Codex Borgia, p. 50.

pochtli in which the eagle, the cactus, and the rock figured as mystic sought-after signs for the place of settlement (Alvarado Tezozmoc 1971: 330–3).

Caso saw the nopal cactus springing directly from the torso of Chalchihuitlicue, after the manner of certain figures in the Codex Borgia (Fig. 23b). His interpretation consequently centered on the meaning of the eagle and cactus as an esoteric expression of the sun-cult. The sun was metaphorically known as *cuauhtlehuanitl*, "ascending eagle," and *cuauhtemoc*, "descending eagle"; sacrificial hearts were *cuauhnochtli*, "cactus fruit of the eagle." The representation of an eagle devouring cactus fruit in the form of stylized human hearts could therefore be taken as a metaphor for the sun-cult. The cactus was interpreted by Caso as a kind of sacrificial tree, supplying sacred food for the sun. This esoteric meaning is certainly acceptable, but it must not obscure the primary meaning of the relief, which is most basically a hieroglyphic representation of the name of Tenochtitlan. After this, the relief is concerned with portraying the historical re-

ality—or at least the legendary historical reality—of the founding of the city. Finally, on an esoteric level of meaning, we may read it for its sun-cult significance, i.e., as a statement of policy and purpose: it was the sacred mission of the warriors of Tenochtitlan to supply the sun with sacrificial victims. As an image of political and religious propaganda, the relief admirably proclaims Mexica aggression as divinely motivated, a motivation which the more realistic inhabitants of the Valley perceived as the very reverse of divine.

The fact that this rear panel represents Tenochtitlan and simultaneously proclaims its mission is supported by the figures carved upon the top of the Teocalli sanctuary (Fig. 22c). The first motif is the date 2-Calli (house), corresponding to the year 1325 when Tenochtitlan was founded. Since Caso (1927) had not found the glyphic name of Tenochtitlan on the rear relief and had instead interpreted the eagle and cactus exclusively in terms of sun-cult symbolism, he rejected 1325 in favor of another 2-Calli date mentioned in

Fig. 24 Varieties of the *tlachinolli* glyph. Left, a ritual impersonator wearing a fire-serpent (*xiuhcoatl*) upon his back. Codex Borbonicus, p. 20. Reproduced with the permission of Akademische Druck- u. Verlagsanstalt, Graz, from the facsimile edition. Right, a fire-serpent from the Sun Stone (after Beyer 1921: Fig. 210). (See also Fig. 22c.)

some sources as the time in which warfare was initiated at the beginning of the present era. A woven-grass hemisphere, set with jeweled awls or ornamented maguey spines, arches over the glyph; this is the familiar penitential artifact we have already described on the Dedication Stone. But it is more elaborate in the present case, for it is crowned by a somewhat enigmatic ritual sign that demands detailed discussion.

To do so we shall return for a moment to the 1-Tecpatl and 1-Miquiztli date glyphs on the sanctuary side panels (Figs. 22e and f). Both glyphs are adorned with plumed and jeweled diadems set with the same curious device, each differing slightly in detail. These ensembles have been interpreted as emblems of Tezcatlipoca: *tezcatl*, "mirror" (indicated by the circular diadem), and *poctli*, "smoke" (represented by volutes attached to the shaft of a bone awl set into the center of the mirror). Pairs of eyes, or possibly pieces of jade, are set within the upper curve of these smoke-volutes. The similarity between these signs and the one on the grass hemisphere can readily be seen; the most appreciable difference in the latter is the substitution of the mirror for another, crownlike motif which has been

identified as a variant of the glyph *tlachinolli*, "burnt thing" (compare this crownlike motif with other *tlachinolli* glyphs, Fig. 24). The sanctuary-top relief is completed by two flanking paper torches, elaborately knotted or folded in the form of fire-serpents.

Practically all these motifs occur in one combination or another in association with Tezcatlipoca, Huitzilopochtli, or such figures as Tepeyollotl, "heart of the mountain" (Fig. 25). The motifs in question may have an emblematic value, but in a more general sense they are visual kennings for rulership, authority, wisdom, and command. Sahagún lists several figures of speech illustrating these metaphors:

HE WHO GOETH SMOKING, WHO GOETH BURNING
This saying was said of him who was of very firm speech as he admonished one; and the words hurt one; he spoke not gently. And everyone was sore afraid; no more did one speak aloud; everyone heard him very well. (Sahagún 1951–70, Bk. 6: 252)

SMOKE, MIST; FAME, HONOR
This saying was said of some ruler not long dead, whose smoke, whose mist, had not yet vanished; that is, his honor, his glory; or someone who had gone far away, whose glory,

58

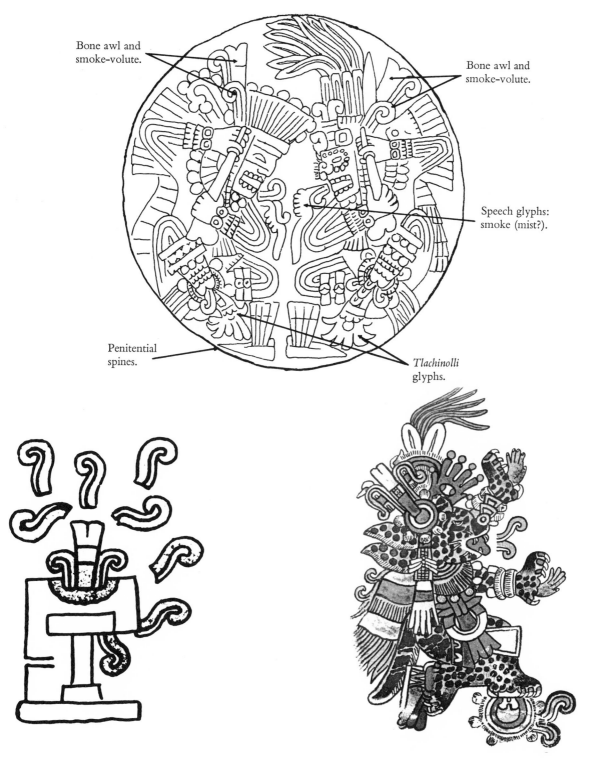

Bone awl and
smoke-volute.

Bone awl and
smoke-volute.

Speech glyphs:
smoke (mist?).

Penitential
spines.

Tlachinolli
glyphs.

Fig. 25 Bone awls, penitential spines, *tlachinolli* glyphs, and signs for smoke or mist. Above, Tezcatlipoca and Huitzilo-pochtli (after Caso 1958: 30). Right, below, Tepeyollotl. Left and right, below, from the Codex Borbonicus, pp. 17, 3. Reproduced with the permission of Akademische Druck- u. Verlagsanstalt, Graz, from the facsimile edition.

whose honor had not yet vanished. (Sahagún 1951–70, Bk. 6: 244)

I LAY BEFORE THEE THE LIGHT, THE TORCH, THE MODEL, THE MEASURE, THE WIDE MIRROR

This saying was said of one who spoke as a nobleman to the common folk. He placed a very good discourse before the common folk. He said to them: "Before you I set up that which is like a torch, like a light. And I place before you that which is like a mirror. Or I give thee thy model, which is like thy measure; from it thou art to take thyself a model, thou art to take thyself an example, in order to live well, or in order to speak well." (Sahagún 1951–70, Bk. 6: 246)

[THE SPINY, THE THORNY]

[Spiny, Thorny] was said of some ruler, or of a nobleman, of one worthy of great honor. No one could draw very near to him: he was considered as a wild beast. Therefore it was said to one who held a ruler not in esteem: "Is it as if thou thinkest the ruler or authority to be thornless? Dost thou consider him to be spineless as thou goest bringing thy complaints before him? Perhaps the continuous complaints trouble the ruler greatly!" (Sahagún 1951–70, Bk. 6: 245)

(Anderson and Dibble translate this as "spineless, thornless"; Rémi Siméon's *Dictionnaire* suggests the translation presented above, which seems to correspond more closely with Sahagún's explanatory text.)

ONE'S HAIR, ONE'S NAILS, ONE'S SPINES, ONE'S THORNS, ONE'S BEARD, ONE'S EYEBROWS, ONE'S CHIP, ONE'S FRAGMENT

It means the one born into the lineage of rulership, the status of nobility. And indeed he was also named "one's blood, one's color." (Sahagún 1951–70, Bk. 6: 245)

Elaborate smoke, mist, and flame motifs are shown as speech-glyphs in reliefs depicting kings (one of whom wears a jaguar-mask upon his back, the other wears a beard, a third is attired as a jaguar) on stone boxes whose purpose has never been accurately identified (Fig. 26). Like the glyphs upon the Teocalli, they surely communicate general ideas concerning honor, fame, good counsel, authority, and nobility. The foundation date of Tenochtitlan atop the Teocalli sanctuary is thus qualified by these motifs to reinforce the dignity of that historical moment.

The final theme of the Teocalli concerns the meaning of the four personages seated in cross-legged posi-

Fig. 26 Regal personages with speech-glyphs from smoke, mist; the uppermost figure also shows *tlachinolli* and penitential spines (after Seler 1902–23, II: 726, 732).

60

tion on the side panels (Fig. 22). Caso (1927) and Palacios (1929) regarded them as gods, though both authors noted articles of priestly attire. Palacios especially remarked on the similarity of these priestly garments to those worn by Tizoc and Ahuizotl on the Dedication Stone. Nevertheless, it was the principal concern of these investigators to identify and interpret the more spectacular headdresses, facial markings, jewelry, and other accessories; on the basis of these items the four personages were identified as: (a) Tlahuizcalpantecuhtli, "dawn lord" (the name of the planet Venus); (b) Tlaloc (according to Durán, the name means "path under the earth" or "long cave" [Durán 1971: 154]; Tlaloc is preeminently associated with water, rain, fertility); (c) Xiuhtecuhtli, "turquoise lord" (an appellation given to the element fire); and (d) Xochipilli, "flower prince" (a name associated with the cults of food plants and also with the pleasures and festivities of palace folk). By Caso's own admission these interpretations were tentative, especially concerning Xochipilli. Palacios made no specific attribution in the latter case, only noting that the headdress with its pleated fan is of a type commonly worn by gods of vegetation and the summer months. Both scholars explained the presence of these figures on the Teocalli in terms of sun-cult mythology, Caso speculating that they were the gods who had assembled to witness the auto-sacrifices that produced the sun and moon at the beginning of the present era, Palacios regarding them as a kind of microcosm of the pantheon, symbolically expressing the subordinate position of the gods in relation to the principal god, i.e., the sun. To reassess these views we shall first direct our attention to the garments of priestly attire which the figures wear, and then to the garments which Caso and Palacios have identified.

The short-sleeved shirts, the copal bags, the backpouches with magical potions, and the maguey leaves set with spines, are indeed the identifying garments of the priesthood, as has already been related. But aside from these basic items, our information on the varieties of priestly garments and their connection with the various offices of the priestly hierarchy is scattered

and incomplete in comparison to the detailed descriptions and pictorial representations of ceremonial impersonators. The problem therefore lies in finding a way of linking the garments of these four personages to some office, or offices, within the priesthood, and then relating our findings to the major themes of the Teocalli.

The priestly hierarchy of Tenochtitlan appears to have been organized under two principal priests called Quequetzalcoa, in memory of Quetzalcoatl, the great legendary civilizer of Toltec times (Acosta Saignes 1946). The entire priesthood was, of course, under the nominal direction of the emperor, as has been related above. Specifically, the two great primates were respectively denominated Tlaloc Totec Tlamacazqui and Quetzalcoatl Totec Tlamacazqui; their headquarters were respectively in the Tlaloc and Huitzilopochtli shrines, which were placed side by side on the platform of the Main Pyramid of Tenochtitlan. These two priests were responsible for the activities of the lower priestly orders.

The Tlaloc priest was in charge of the Tequipane, described as younger priests with many kinds of duties. They have been likened to Deacons in the Christian Church, and seem to have acted as the parish priests of Tenochtitlan. Another office associated with the Tlaloc priest was that of Tlalocan Tlenamacac, the censer of the Tlaloc temple; also associated with the Tlaloc priest was Epcoacuaquiltzin, who was the coordinator and master of religious ceremonies at Tenochtitlan:

The Epcoacuaquiltzin—behold what were his duties: when feasts should be celebrated, perchance when a new fifty-two-year cycle should start—verily, all feasts—all of them he announced; or when fire was laid. In truth, all that should be done, all things this man thus commanded and furthered. (Sahagún 1951–70, Bk. 2: 194)

Quetzalcoatl Totec Tlamacazqui was primarily connected with the Huitzilopochtli cult, despite the seemingly anomalous title. The name Quetzalcoatl was simply a holdover of a traditional title which in earlier times and among older nations had been given to the high priest. For example, one of the two main priests at Chollolan was known by this venerable title. Quetzalcoatl Totec Tlamacazqui was charged with the supervision of the senior priesthood, the Tlenamacaque, who saw to the censing of war prisoners and returning warriors, the censing of the stars and the moon by night, and the distribution of new fire. (The "censing" involved much more than the burning of incense, which was only one aspect of the complex rituals for which these priests were responsible.) The keeper of the Copoloc temple who was especially charged with creating new fire was a Tlenamacaque priest. These senior priests also gave public sermons and addresses concerning the need to go to war or to attend the cultivated fields. Still another title associated with the Quetzalcoatl priest was Teopixcatiachcau, whose duties concerned the administration of the warrior priests who accompanied military expeditions and personally participated in armed combat.

There were also many ceremonies in which special priests officiated, but their ultimate affiliations in the two main branches of the religious hierarchy are uncertain. Among these were the Cuetlaxteca, who were primarily responsible for carrying out sacrificial duties.

Before returning to the Teocalli figures, let us review some passages from Sahagún describing the New Fire ceremonies as they were held in the year 2-Acatl, 1507. It will be remembered that the dates 1-Tochtli (the last year of the old 52-year cycle) and 2-Acatl (the beginning of the new cycle) are carved on the lower balustrades of the Teocalli. The fact that they represent the "binding of the years" which this cyclically recurring ceremony marked has been established not only by correlations of the native and Christian calendar systems (Caso 1971: Table 5), but also by the fact that the 2-Acatl glyph is shown with a small rope tied around the middle.

At nightfall, from here in Mexico, they departed. All the fire priests were arranged in order, arrayed in and wearing the garb of the gods. Each one represented and was the likeness of perhaps Quetzalcoatl, or Tlaloc, etc., or whichever one he went representing. Very deliberately, very stately, they proceeded, went spread out, and slowly moved. It was said: "They walk like gods." Thus, in deep night, they arrived there at Uixachtlan.

And the one who was the fire priest of Copulco, who drew new fire, then began there. With his hands he proceeded to bore continuously his fire drill. . . .

And when it came to pass that night fell, all were frightened and filled with dread. Thus it was said: it was claimed that if fire could not be drawn, then [the sun] would be destroyed forever; all would be ended; there would evermore be night. Nevermore would the sun come forth. . . .

. . . .

Hence was heed paid only one thing; there was unwavering attention and expectation as all remained facing, with neck craned, the summit of Uixachtecatl. Everyone was apprehensive, waiting until, in time, the new fire might be drawn—until, in good time [a flame] would burst forth and shine out. And when a little came forth, when it took fire, lit, and blazed, then it flared and burst into flames, and was visible everywhere. It was seen from afar. (Sahagún 1951–70, Bk. 7: 27–8)

Following this, relay runners sped from the mountaintop to distribute the fire to all the surrounding towns and to all the temples of Tenochtitlan. Alvarado Tezozomoc, describing the same ceremony, mentions that this distribution was carried out by the Tlenamacaque and that it ceased with the appearance of the morning star (Alvarado Tezozomoc 1944: 467–8). Sacrifices were naturally featured during the ceremony and more sacrifices followed later in the day at the Xiuhtecuhtli temple. This new fire was a symbol of regeneration, of the rebirth of time, and in this respect the ceremony can be seen as a reenactment or a re-creation of the time of genesis. But in addition to this metaphysical significance it symbolized the renewal of the existing social order for another 52-year cycle.

It seems reasonable to regard the four enigmatic personages on the Teocalli sides as members of the priestly orders involved in the New Fire ceremonies, though the evidence is largely circumstantial. There is a Tlaloc-associated figure, doubtlessly linked to the hierarchy of Tlaloc Totec Tlamacazqui in some capacity. Tlahuizcalpantecuhtli, Venus, is mentioned prominently in descriptions of the new fire distribution ceremony. The observation of Venus was important in astronomy and chronology, for a cycle of 65 Venusian years equalled 104 solar years, that is, two 52-year cycles, a long period called *huehuelitztli*, "an old age." At the end of this period the new beginning of the solar and Venusian cycles coincided, and Sahagún's description of the Binding of the Years leads us to believe that the new fire ceremonies held at Uixachtlan in 1507 was just such an occasion (Sahagún 1951–70, Bk. 7: 25). One last detail of the priest with *tlahuizcalpantecuhtli* attire concerns the tied leather arm and legbands: the word for leather is *cuetlaxtli*, which suggests that these bands may be emblematic of sacrificial duties (priests specializing in sacrifice were called Cuetlaxteca). Xiuhtecuhtli, the metaphoric name for fire, is repeatedly mentioned in connection with the new fire ceremonies. Only the putative Xochipilli priest-impersonator remains unaccounted for and cannot be identified with greater precision at the present time. Again, this interpretation is tentative—another possible line of investigation might establish connections between these priestly figures and the four quarters of Tenochtitlan.

The pyramidal form of the Teocalli represents the sacred nature of Tenochtitlan, whose foundation, subsequent alliances, imperial aspirations, and hopes for perpetuation were systematically represented by the sculptural reliefs. The Teocalli was fashioned some eighty-odd years after the Mexica nation had embarked on a policy of imperial expansion. Within that remarkable space of time a uniquely Mexica system of habits and thoughts had formed and was visually translated on a series of commemorative sculptures, of which the Teocalli is an especially complex example. Although sculptural monuments vary in complexity, their symbolic elements describe the same perception of the world and display consistent structural relationships. Borrowing selectively from the repertory of existing artistic traditions, the Mexica created a commonly held visual language in which cosmological symbols conjoined with those of historical events to define the position of Tenochtitlan as the legitimate heir to the wealth, power, holiness, and sovereignty of Mesoamerica.

The "Sun Stone": Time, Space, and the Ascendancy of Tenochtitlan

Discovered beneath the downtown plaza of Mexico City in 1790, this large (3.60 meters, diameter), intricately carved disc has been a major subject of scholarly debate since the nineteenth century (Fig. 27). Undoubtedly it once occupied a prominent position somewhere in the main ceremonial center of Tenochtitlan, but the name and location of the building where it was originally placed have not been definitively traced. Another related question also remains unanswered: was this sculpture fixed vertically to a wall, as it has been traditionally displayed in the National Museum of Anthropology, or was it set into a floor, perhaps as the center of a circular shrine akin to the Pantheon of Rome, or the Dome of the Rock in Jerusalem? It is beyond the scope of the present study to review the complex architectural data on the ceremonial center, but the question of vertical or horizontal positioning has a suggestive bearing on the immediate problem of iconographic interpretation, as we shall see on following pages.

Of all the scholarly articles devoted to deciphering the sculptural relief, Beyer's (1921) analysis is the most widely accepted and has remained essentially unmodified until the present time. It was Beyer's theory that all the iconographical motifs refer to the sun (1) as it was metaphorically conceived as a time-period (an era), and (2) as it was worshiped as a physical source of heat and life. Since the publication of Beyer's work the sculpture has thus been popularly regarded as a cult object dedicated to the sun, a view which Caso championed in his later work (Caso 1958). I shall briefly summarize Beyer's argument in order to place it in the perspective afforded by the commemorative monuments discussed above, for, like these other monuments, the Sun Stone may be read on many levels.

Beyer (1921) regarded the anthropomorphic mask at the center of the disc as the face of the sun-god Tonatiuh, basing his interpretation on the comparison of several images taken from Post-Conquest codices. Clawed hands clutching human hearts flank this cen-

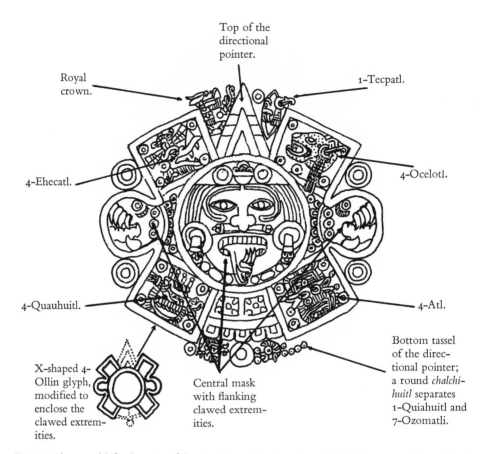

Top of the directional pointer.

Royal crown.

1-Tecpatl.

4-Ehecatl.

4-Ocelotl.

4-Quauhuitl.

4-Atl.

Bottom tassel of the directional pointer; a round *chalchihuitl* separates 1-Quiahuitl and 7-Ozomatli.

X-shaped 4-Ollin glyph, modified to enclose the clawed extremities.

Central mask with flanking clawed extremities.

Fig. 27 Above and left, elements of the Sun Stone (line drawings after Noriega 1954: Frontispiece).

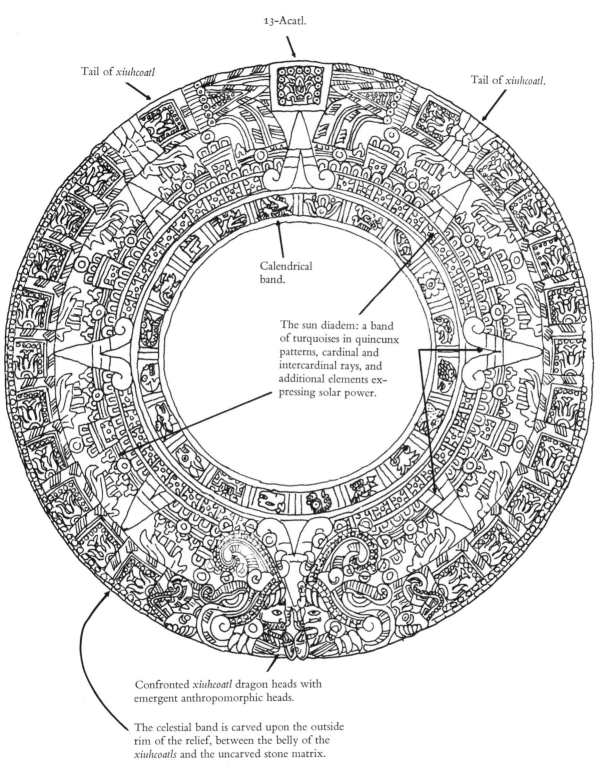

13-Acatl.

Tail of *xiuhcoatl*

Tail of *xiuhcoatl*.

Calendrical band.

The sun diadem: a band of turquoises in quincunx patterns, cardinal and intercardinal rays, and additional elements expressing solar power.

Confronted *xiuhcoatl* dragon heads with emergent anthropomorphic heads.

The celestial band is carved upon the outside rim of the relief, between the belly of the *xiuhcoatls* and the uncarved stone matrix.

65

tral visage: these were interpreted as eagle talons, evoking the sun's metaphoric appellations *cuauhtlehua-nitl*, "ascending eagle," *cuauhtemoc*, "descending eagle," and the term for sacrificial hearts, *cuauhnochtli*, "cactus fruit of the eagle." These motifs are enclosed by a linear X-shaped frame set with four large dots—two to the left, and two to the right, bracketing the protruding talons. This is the sign of 4-Ollin, "4-Earthquake," or "4-Movement," the date on which the present era in Mexica time was to be destroyed by earthquakes: thus the mask in combination with the encircling sun-diadem was to be read as *ollintonatiuh*, "earthquake-sun" (or "movement-sun"). Glyphs representing the four preceeding ages are set into the arms of the X-shaped frame. Reading them in counter-clockwise order, they are, respectively, 4-Ocelotl (an ocelot's head; that era was said to have ended when a population of giants was destroyed by ocelots or jaguars), 4-Ehecatl (the wind-mask; this era was thought to have ended in hurricanes), 4-Quauhuitl (a Tlaloc mask signifying an era which was supposed to have ended in a fiery rain), and 4-Atl (a Chalchihui-tlicue mask in a basin, symbolizing an era that ended in floods). Thus, the names of the former suns were taken from the dates on which they perished, and the name of the present sun is that of the predicted time of its destruction. In Beyer's estimation, the four small glyphs placed just outside the linear frame were associated with the four directions. Beginning at the top, and moving in counterclockwise order, these signs are: 1-Tecpatl (the date 1-Stone Knife), a royal diadem with a lip plug and a smoke glyph, 1-Quiahuitl (the date 1-Water), and 7-Ozomatli (the date 7-Monkey). The last motif of this central ensemble is a triangular point separating 1-Tecpatl and the royal diadem; this point must be seen in conjunction with the decorated fringe hanging below, just above the 1-Quiahuitl and 7-Ozomatli dates—similar arrangements shown in codices indicate that it is an arrow, or pointer. Beyer remained somewhat at a loss for an explanation for this curious compasslike motif.

Next to be examined is the calendrical band which encloses the central ensemble, separating it from the sun-diadem. The twenty day signs of the native month are read in counterclockwise order, beginning at the top with *cipactli*, "alligator," or "crocodile," and ending with *xochitl*, "flower." These signs refer to the passage of time (they are also the source of the name "Calendar Stone," by which this monument is also popularly known).

Next in the sequence of concentric rings is the sun-diadem itself, set with a profusion of jade and turquoise symbols as a way of indicating precious quality. Like the diadem atop the Stone of Tizoc, this solar emblem shoots out rays to the cardinal and intercardinal directions.

Finally, two dragonlike *xiuhcoatls* ("fire serpents") parenthetically enclose the sun: their tails meet above at a cartouche with the date 13-Acatl, and their open jaws with emerging anthropomorphic faces are confronted below. These faces were identified by Beyer as Tonatiuh, "sun" (left), and Xiuhtecuhtli, "turquoise lord" (right). Xiuhtecuhtli was a metaphoric name for fire; "turquoise" was here again used to convey the notion of something precious. Beyer remarked that Tonatiuh likenesses rarely combine with *xiuhcoatls* in Mexica sculpture, but that there is ample precedent in earlier Mesoamerican art for sun-related figures emerging from the mouths of dragons, especially in Classic Maya art. The igneous associations of the *xiuhcoatl* torches carved upon the Teocalli have already been briefly mentioned, and it may be added that impersonators dressed in Xiuhtecuhtli attire frequently appeared with fire-serpents upon their backs in the rituals of Tenochtitlan (Fig. 28). As early as 1908 Beyer speculated that *xiuhcoatls* represented the heat, luminosity, and vivid blue of the daytime sky, and he later observed that *xiuhcoatls* were probably conceived as mythological creatures with the assigned role of transporting the sun across the sky on its daily path. The 13-Acatl glyph was interpreted by Beyer as the date of the present sun's creation; in this he followed an earlier suggestion of Seler's, as well as the creation legends mentioned in such sources as the *Anales de Cuauhtitlan* (Ramírez 1885) and the *Historia de los Mexicanos por sus Pinturas* (1941).

Fig. 28 Seated Xiuhtecuhtli impersonator pierces his ear (after Beyer 1921: Fig. 205).

The final element of the monument is a celestial band representing the star-strewn night sky. This is carved on the outside rim of the disc, separating it from the uncarved stone matrix. Like the similar starry band around the Stone of Tizoc, it completes the picture of the heavenly sphere. This concludes Beyer's interpretation of the Sun Stone, which is by all accounts the most iconographically complex monument of Mexica art thus far recovered. In Beyer's estimation all the elements of the composition could be related to the sun, as it was conceived as a symbol of the present era, and as it was worshiped as a god of life and life-giving heat.

But we cannot forget that the Mexica felt the need to assert the validity of their state to their contemporaries as well as to themselves, and that sculptural art communicated these concerns in direct, explicit fashion that left no room for doubt. Therefore it may be surmised that a monument as ambitious as the Sun Stone would make some direct reference to the Mexica state. To set Beyer's argument in the perspective afforded by the other monuments we have seen, let us recall the mosaic shield and the Stone of Tizoc: both are cosmograms with circular shape, and both have motifs indicating the horizontal and vertical divisions of the cosmos. Could the Sun Stone similarly be a "compressed" cosmogram, intended to be set

into a floor? Here we return to the argument for a horizontal, as opposed to a vertical position. Curiously, Beyer thought it had probably been displayed horizontally, though not for the same reasons that we shall be concerned with.

The question can be resolved by pointing out that the supposed eagle claws flanking the central mask are really more akin to the five-clawed gloves worn by Tlaltecuhtli and related impersonators (Figs. 12, 13, 14, 15). In effect, eagle talons have only four claws, a detail not likely to have been glossed over on this major monument. Seler (1902–23, II: 790) had also observed that the five-clawed gloves suggested jaguar paws, and that the jaguar was an animal traditionally associated with the earth; but Beyer (1921) contested this idea by pointing to a Mictlantecuhtli ("lord of the land of the dead") figure from the Post-Conquest Magliabecchiano Codex, shown with four-clawed birdlike talons (Fig. 29). Mictlantecuhtli is certainly associated with the earth, and Beyer argued that there was therefore no particular consistency in the number of claws depicted on these images; a five-clawed glove could just as well have served to represent the solar eagle. The argument is unconvincing, for iconographic inconsistencies are more easily apt to occur in Post-Conquest manuscripts than on a monument of the caliber of the Sun Stone. It is highly probable that the five-clawed gloves flanking the central mask do in fact refer to Tlaltecuhtli, and not to the eagle as a sun metaphor. This becomes evident when the mask is compared to similar masks on Tlaltecuhtli effigies (see especially Figs. 12, 13) and when the flanking position of the gloves is seen in relation to the impersonator's ritual posture of holding the hands upon, or just in front of, the shoulders. The idea that the central mask of the Sun Stone represents the *face of the earth*, and not the face of Tonatiuh, "the sun," is consistent with the enclosing glyph *ollin*. Was it not predicted that the present sun would end in earthquakes, the "movement of the earth?" Moreover, the presence of a Tlaltecuhtli mask is consistent with the iconography of the other commemorative monuments we have seen —and like the Tlaltecuhtli images on the Dedication

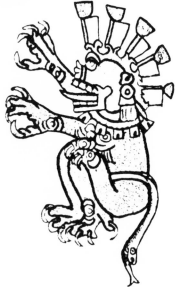

Fig. 29 Above, fragment of a Tlaltecuhtli with characteristic five-clawed footwear. Photo courtesy of the Museo Nacional de Antropología, Mexico. Right, a four-clawed Mictlante-cuhtli, Codex Magliabecchiano, p. 79. Reproduced with the permission of Akademische Druck- u. Verlagsanstalt, Graz, from the facsimile edition.

Stone, the Stone of Tizoc, and the Teocalli, it may also be interpreted as representing both the sacred earth and the territory of the Mexica nation.

Cem anahuac Tenochca tlalpan, "the world, Tenochca (Mexica) land": does this interpretation of the central mask correlate with the rest of the Sun Stone iconography? We may begin by re-examining the four small glyphs which Beyer thought to be esoteric signs for the four directions. With the large rays of the sun already clearly establishing the cardinal and intercardinal directions, what other meaning could these small glyphs have? The first of them, 1-Tecpatl, has been explained as the calendar date of Huitzilopochtli on the Teocalli. Next is the royal diadem with lip plug and a speech-glyph in the shape of an abbreviated sign for smoke or mist (also note the small breastplate of the type worn by warriors below). This assembly refers to the office of Mexica kingship, and communicates its might, fame, and honor. The two bottom glyphs, 1-Atl and 7-Ozomatli, are, like 1-Tecpatl, the names of days in the 260-day divinatory cycle, the *tonalpohualli*; however, the cults to which these two days were ritually dedicated remain somewhat enigmatic (no full account of the ritual cycles and the movable ceremonies using all the primary sources has yet appeared). Nevertheless the day 1-Atl is mentioned as being dedicated to Chalchihuitlicue, and was observed by those who gained their lives in aquatic pursuits. Most probably this cult was of very ancient origin among the lakeshore peoples, and it may have reached Tenochtitlan from one of its allied cities—Tlacopan, for instance. One may speculate that the 7-Ozomatli has similar ritual and sociopolitical implications as the day of the cult of an important community within Tenochtitlan or within an allied city. However incomplete, this reassessment of the four small glyphs indicates that they fall into the general pattern of signs and symbols that we have seen on other commemorative monuments, in that they illustrate matters of immediate historical importance to the Mexica state.

Next to be considered is cosmological orientation, a topic that has already been touched upon in men-tioning the counterclockwise reading of the calendrical band and the disposition of the sun rays. It will be recalled that in the Indian frame of reference, the cardinal points were customarily described from a dominant position facing east; and that the north, west, and south quadrants followed in that order. It is therefore to be supposed that the most important region, the eastern place of life, light, and authority, would be emphasized in cosmological compositions. In the present case, east is undoubtedly at the top of the monument, in the position that would normally be assigned to the north in the current European system of orientation. The primacy of east is not only expressed by (1) the counterclockwise movement of the calendrical band which begins at the "top" with the glyph *cipactli*, but also by (2) the compass-like "pointer" that Beyer could not account for, (3) the direction of the dragonlike *xiuhcoatls*, and (4) the significance of the 13-Acatl date.

The curious triangular "pointer" with its elaborately decorated tassel at last becomes meaningful when seen as a directional arrow on the surface of the earth, pointing to the place of the sun's emergence. Read in terms of its association with the other glyphs in this central portion of the Sun Stone, it expresses metaphorically an inseparable association between the earth as Mexica territory, the royal house and official cult of Tenochtitlan, and the sacred (east) place of cosmological authority.

Beyer believed that the two dragonlike *xiuhcoatls* represented mythological animals associated with the celestial sphere, whose task it was to bear the sun across the sky. This interpretation cannot be contested in any major way save to point out that the *xiuhcoatls* should be seen as metaphoric pictograms—as opposed to mythological creatures—of the heat, light, and color of the sky. The notion that they are connected with the path of the sun appears to be borne out by their "downward" movement from the 13-Acatl cartouche; like the "serpent balustrades" that flank the stairways of so many Mesoamerican pyramids, they express the flow of energy or power from one place to the next. And in this respect, their cosmological meaning can be metaphorically correlated with the power of the Mexica nation. This is illustrated by Sahagún's description of the annual Panquetzalitztli festivals, held in honor of Huitzilopochtli; in a concluding episode of the ritual events, a large paper-and-feather *xiuh-coatl* was brought down the steps from the platform of the Main Pyramid, to be presented at an altar on the bottom landing:

Thereupon likewise descended the fire serpent, looking like a blazing pine firebrand. Its tongue was made of red arara feathers, looking like a flaming torch. And its tail was of paper, two or three fathoms long. As it descended, it came moving its tongue, like that of a real serpent, darting in and out.

And when [the priest] had come [with it], bringing it down to the base [of the pyramid], he proceeded carefully to the eagle vessel. Then he went up [to the eagle vessel] and raised [the fire serpent] also to the four directions. When he had [so] raised it up, then he cast it upon the sacrificial paper, and then they burned. (Sahagún 1951–70, Bk. 2: 136)

Celestial luminosity, heat, and the generative might of the sun are metaphorically represented by this dragon-like creature; through the east-west orientation of the pyramid, these powers are shown to originate in the direction of the sun's emergence and are brought down to the surface of the earth and presented to the four directions. By analogy, Huitzilopochtli and his chosen people were recognized in terms of these celestial forces.

The last main element of the Sun Stone to account for is the date-glyph 13-Acatl. There can be no doubt about the mythological importance of this date, for it is mentioned in at least two versions of the origin myth as the time of the present sun's creation. Yet the glyph also reoccurs in the calendar cycle to mark a more directly historical year of genesis: 1427, the year of Itzcoatl's accession to power and the cruel beginning of an imperial vision, a time in which the Mexica began to conceive of themselves as great, and to create a sense of historical mission that propelled Tenochtitlan from the position of a backwater tributary city to a position of unparalleled might in Mesoamerica. By illustrating the conjunction of a cyclically recurring date in sacred time with the time of national independence and the first territorial aggrandizement, the rulers of Tenochtitlan sanctified the authority of their imperial office. Placed in the cardinal position of supreme importance, 13-Acatl acts as a validating touchstone linking the cosmic and the social orders.

More than any other single monument, the Sun Stone demonstrates how the vitality and the structure of the natural order were conceived of as models, indeed were automatically equated with the activities and the organization of society. The four quarters of the earth and an imperial territory; divine patronage, imperial sovereignty, and the direction east; the calendar, the present solar era, and Mexica rule; and the generative force of the sun and the might of the Mexica nation—all are inseparably associated in this sculptural relief. In the Mexica vision of the world, the hard aims of secular power were fused with a fundamentally mythopoeic outlook in which every aspect of life was part of a cosmic system. In such a system, the universe was seen as a reflection of relationships between life-forces. In that immensely magic world, perceived objects were automatically translated into another level: the boundaries between objective and perceptive become blurred, dream and reality are one, and everything is alive and intimately relatable.

Conclusions

Interpretation of the Mexica monuments is an indispensable step in reconstructing the ideological world of Mesoamerican civilization, but the problems of disjunction and continuity must be kept in mind if these monuments are to be used as effective points of departure in understanding earlier traditions. Three basic themes have emerged in examining the cult effigies and historical commemorative monuments: first, the fact that the universe was conceived as a sacred structure; second, the fact that the social order and the territory of the nation were seen to correspond with this cosmic structure; and third, the fact that Tenochtitlan was represented as the triumphant, sovereign, and historically legitimate successor to the civilization of the past. Cult effigies embodied community and national identity and, as instruments of imperial policy, they were used to confirm political alliances; held in the *coateocalli* of Tenochtitlan, they also acted as magical hostages for the cult identity of tributary nations. But behind these immediate political uses peculiar to the Mexica empire, there lay a deeper ideological underpinning: these images also portrayed the universe as it was conceived in terms of living, hallowed powers, and commemorated the traditional cult offices of living and ancestral leaders in maintaining the connection between community and cosmos. Historical commemorative monuments recorded the decisive events of Mexica national history—as it was officially interpreted according to imperial policy—and celebrated the role of kings, priests, and other major functionaries of the Mexica social hierarchy. But these events and offices could only be meaningful when legitimized by portraying them symbolically in cosmological settings; the state and the social order were only valid and therefore understandable in the measure that they were equated with the sacred world.

Mexica sculpture transmits information on two levels. The first concerns the unique history, policy, and socioeconomic structure of the Mexica state, and the second concerns the validation of that state in relation to a larger universal whole. The first level of information is more transitory and disjunctive with the past, for it concerns specifically Mexica events and institutions. It is on the second level that we find a matrix of ideas transcending the imperial preoccupations of Tenochtitlan. These ideas provide continuity between the Mexica people and their predecessors.

A few brief examples will indicate this continuity. To begin with, we have already noted that cosmological symbolism was handed down to the Mexica via the conservative Postclassic Mixteca-Puebla manuscript tradition. In Classic Maya art, cosmic symbols were associated with dynastic rulers, as insignia (Fig. 30) and as settings (Fig. 31) in many kinds of scenes. In Preclassic Izapa art, a fixed vocabulary of cosmic symbols formed a validating frame of reference for the specialized activities of socioeconomic groups, as in the "fisherman" stela, which depicts a ritually attired personage netting fish between river (or sea) and sky (Fig. 32). Among the Preclassic Olmecs, regal personages are depicted emerging from cavelike niches surmounted with vegetal motifs and jaguar-masks (Fig. 33). These "altars" probably symbolize the theme of the emergence of a tribal ancestral hero—or the tribe itself as a collective entity—from the heart of the earth, a widespread episode in the genesis stories of many Indian peoples. Each of these cultures differed in socio-economic structure, and each evolved in different places and historical circumstances, but all were as concerned as the Mexica to validate their social order by representing its connection with the hallowed universe. Cosmic signs and symbols changed in time and place, yet it would be difficult to speak of totally different religious systems. Rather, Mesoamerican iconography displays a pattern of synthesis, dissolution, and resynthesis of a basic inventory of cosmic themes, indicating the persistence of a world view in which all aspects of life were integrated by the essentially religious recognition of oneness between the natural and the social orders.

Fig. 30 Palenque, Temple of the Sun, sanctuary tablet. At center, a shield with jaguar-sun face is suspended from crossed ceremonial spears. Drawing by Linda Schele.

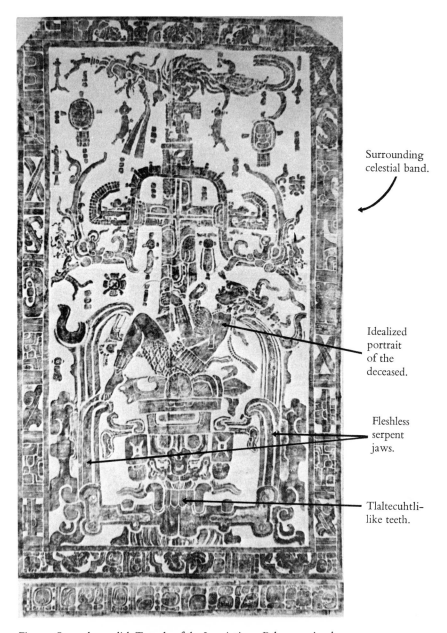

Surrounding celestial band.

Idealized portrait of the deceased.

Fleshless serpent jaws.

Tlaltecuhtli– like teeth.

Fig. 31 Sarcophagus lid, Temple of the Inscriptions, Palenque. A celestial band surrounds a scene in which the deceased is borne into the sky in the fleshless jaws of an earth–serpent (note Tlaltecuhtli–like teeth, bottom center). Rubbing by Merle Greene Robertson.

Conventionalized
sky symbol.

Ritual impersonator
holding net with fish;
water pours from this
container.

Ground line, with
river (seashore?).

Fig. 32 The Fisherman Stela (Stela 1) from Izapa. Photo courtesy of
the Museo Nacional de Antropología, Mexico.

74

Fig. 33 Altar 4, La Venta.

Bibliography

ACOSTA SAIGNES, MIGUEL

1946   Los Teopixque. *Revista Mexicana de Estudios Antropológicos*, tomo 8, nos. 1, 2, 3, pp. 147–205. Sociedad Mexicana de Antropología, Mexico.

ALVA IXTLILXOCHITL, FERNANDO DE

1891–92   Obras Históricas. Publicadas y anotadas por Alfredo Chavero. 2 vols. Oficina Tip. de la Secretaría de Fomento, Mexico. (Reprint 1952: Editorial Salvador Chávez Hayhoe, Mexico.)

ALVARADO TEZOZOMOC, FERNANDO

1944   Crónica Mexicana. Editorial Leyenda, Mexico.

1971   The Finding and Founding of Mexico Tenochtitlan: From the *Crónica Mexicayotl*. (Trans. by Thelma D. Sullivan.) *Tlalocan*, vol. VI, no. 4, pp. 312–336. La Casa de Tlaloc, Mexico.

BARLOW, R. H.

1949   The Extent of the Empire of the Culhua Mexica. *Ibero-Americana*: 28. University of California Press, Berkeley and Los Angeles.

BEYER, HERMANN

1908   Der "Drache" der Mexikaner. *Globus*, Bd. XCIII, Nr. 10, pp. 157–158. Braunschweig.

1921   El llamado "Calendario Azteca": descripción e interpretación del cuauhxicalli de la "Casa de las Águilas." Verband Deutscher Reichsangehöriger, Mexico.

CARMICHAEL, ELIZABETH

1970   Turquoise Mosaics from Mexico. Trustees of the British Museum, London.

CARRASCO, PEDRO PIZANA

1950   Los Otomíes: cultura e historia prehispánicas de los pueblos mesoamericanos de habla otomiana. Instituto de Historia, Universidad Nacional Autónoma de México, en colaboración con el Instituto Nacional de Antropología e Historia, Mexico.

CASO, ALFONSO

1927   El Teocalli de la Guerra Sagrada. Publicaciones de la Secretaría de Educación Pública, Monografías del Museo Nacional de Arqueología, Historia y Etnografía. Talleres Gráficos de la Nación, Mexico.

1936   La Religión de los Aztecas. Imprenta Mundial, Mexico.

1939   La Correlación de los Años Azteca y Cristiana. *Revista Mexicana de Estudios Antropológicos*, tomo III, no. 11, pp. 11–45. Sociedad Mexicana de Antropología, Mexico.

1958   The Aztecs: People of the Sun. (Illus. by Miguel Covarrubias, trans. by Lowell Dunham.) University of Oklahoma Press, Norman.

1971   Calendrical Systems of Central Mexico. *In* Handbook of Middle American Indians, vol. 10, part 1, pp. 333–348. University of Texas Press, Austin.

CODEX BORBONICUS

1974   Codex Borbonicus. Bibliothèque de L'Assemblée Nationale – Paris (Y 120). Vollständige FaksimileAusgabe des Codex im Original-format. Kommentar von Karl Anton Nowotny und Jacqueline de Durand-Forest. *Codices Selecti*, vol. XLIV. Akademische Druck- u. Verlagsanstalt, Graz.

CODEX BORGIA

1963   Códice Borgia. Comentarios por Eduard Seler. 3 vols. Fondo de Cultura Económica, Mexico.

CODEX MAGLIABECHIANO

1970   Codex Magliabechiano. CL. XIII. 3 (B.R. 232). Biblioteca Nazionale Centrale di Firenze. Einleitung Summary und Resumen von Ferdinand Anders. *Codices Selecti*, vol. XXIII. Akademische Druck- u. Verlagsanstalt, Graz.

CODEX MENDOCINO

1925   Colección de Mendoza o Códice Mendocino. Documento Mexicano del siglo XVI que se conserva en la Biblioteca Bodleiana de Oxford, Inglaterra. Facsimile Fototípico por Don Francisco del Paso y Troncoso. Talleres Gráficos del Museo Nacional de Arqueología, Historia y Etnografía, Mexico.

COE, MICHAEL D.

1973   The Iconology of Olmec Art. *In* The Iconography of Middle American Sculpture, pp. 1–12. The Metropolitan Museum of Art, New York.

DÍAZ DEL CASTILLO, BERNAL

1904   Historia Verdadera de la Conquista de la Neuva España (Genaro García, ed.). 2 vols. Oficina Tipográfica de la Secretaría de Fomento, Mexico.

1910   The true history of the conquest of New Spain, vol. 3. (Trans. by Alfred Percival Maudslay.) *Works issued by the Hakluyt Society*, 2nd series, vol. XXV. The Hakluyt Society, London.

DURÁN, FRAY DIEGO

1963   Atlas de la historia de las Indias de Nueva España y Islas de Tierra Firme. Librería Anticuaria, G. M. Echaniz, Mexico.

1964   The Aztecs: The History of the Indies of New

Spain. (Trans. by Doris Heyden and Fernando Horcasitas.) Orion Press, New York.

1971 Book of the Gods and Rites and the Ancient Calendar. (Trans. by Fernando Horcasitas and Doris Heyden.) University of Oklahoma Press, Norman.

FERNÁNDEZ, JUSTINO

1954 Coatlicue: Estética del Arte Indígena Antiguo. Instituto de Investigaciones Estéticas, Universidad Nacional Autónoma de México, Mexico.

GRABAR, OLEG

1973 The Formation of Islamic Art. Yale University Press, New Haven.

HISTORIA DE LOS MEXICANOS POR SUS PINTURAS

1941 Historia de los mexicanos por sus pinturas. *In* Nueva colección de documentos para la historia de México. (J. García Icazbalceta, ed.), vol. 3, pp. 207–240. 2nd edition. Mexico.

HISTOYRE DU MÉCHIQUE

1905 Manuscrit français inédit du XVIe siècle. (Publié par M. Edouard de Jonghe.) *Journal de la Société des Américanistes*, n.s. tome II, pp. 1-41. Paris.

HVIDTFELDT, ARILD

1958 Teotl and Ixiptlatli: Some Central Conceptions in Ancient Mexican Religion, with a General Introduction on Cult and Myth. Munksgaard, Copenhagen.

KUBLER, GEORGE

1948 Mexican Architecture of the Sixteenth Century. Yale University Press, New Haven.

1962 The Art and Architecture of Ancient America: The Mexican, Maya, and Andean Peoples. Penguin Books, Baltimore.

1967 The Iconography of the Art of Teotihuacán. *Studies in Pre-Columbian Art and Archaeology*, no. 4. Dumbarton Oaks, Washington.

1969 Studies in Classic Maya Iconography. *Memoirs of the Connecticut Academy of Arts and Sciences*, vol. XVIII. New Haven.

1970 Period, Style and Meaning in Ancient American Art. *New Literary History*, vol. 1, no. 2, pp. 127–144. University of Virginia, Charlottesville.

1973 Science and Humanism among Americanists. *In* The Iconography of Middle American Sculpture, pp. 163–167. The Metropolitan Museum of Art, New York.

LEÓN-PORTILLA, MIGUEL

1963 Aztec Thought and Culture: A Study of the Ancient Nahuatl Mind. (Trans. by Jack Emory Davis.) University of Oklahoma Press, Norman.

1966 La Filosofía Náhuatl: Estudiada en sus Fuentes. Instituto de Investigaciones Históricas, Universidad Nacional Autónoma de México, Mexico.

MACANDREW, JOHN

1965 The Open-Air Churches of Sixteenth-Century Mexico: Atrios, Posas, Open Chapels, and Other Studies. Harvard University Press, Cambridge.

MARTÍNEZ, JOSÉ LUIS

1972 Nezahualcóyotl: Vida y Obra. Fondo de Cultura Económica, Mexico.

MAUDSLAY, ALFRED P.

1909 Plano hecho en papel de maguey que se conserva en el Museo Nacional de México. *Anales del Museo Nacional de México*, época III, tomo I, núm. 2, pp. 49–58. Mexico.

MENDIETA, FRAY GERÓNIMO DE

1945 Historia eclesiástica indiana. 4 vols. Editorial Salvador Chávez Hayhoe, Mexico.

MOTOLINÍA, FRAY TORIBIO DE BENAVENTE

1951 History of the Indians of New Spain. (Trans. by Francis Borgia Steck.) Academy of American Franciscan History, Washington.

MUÑOZ CAMARGO, DIEGO

1947 Historia de Tlaxcala. 6th edition. Universidad Nacional Autónoma de México, Mexico.

NICHOLSON, HENRY B.

1961 The Chapultepec Cliff Sculpture of Motecuhzoma Xocoyotzin. *El México Antiguo*, tomo IX, pp. 379–444. Sociedad Alemana Mexicanista, Mexico.

1967 A fragment of an Aztec relief carving of the Earth Monster. *Journal de la Société des Américanistes*, tome LVI-1, pp. 81–94. Paris.

1971a Major Sculpture in Pre-Hispanic Central Mexico. *In* Handbook of Middle American Indians (Robert Wauchope, Gordon F. Ekholm, and Ignacio Bernal, eds.), vol. 10, Archaeology of Northern Mesoamerica, pt. 1, pp. 92–134. University of Texas Press, Austin.

1971b Religion in Pre-Hispanic Central Mexico. *In* Handbook of Middle American Indians (Robert Wauchope, Gordon F. Ekholm, and Ignacio Bernal, eds.), vol. 10, Archaeology of Northern Mesoamerica, pt. 1, pp. 395-446. University of Texas Press, Austin.

1973 The Late Pre-Hispanic Central Mexican (Aztec) Iconographic System. *In* The Iconography of Middle American Sculpture. The Metropolitan Museum of Art, New York.

NORIEGA, RAÚL

1954 Tres Estudios sobre la Piedra del Sol. Mexico.

OROZCO Y BERRA, MANUEL

1877a El cuauhxicalli de Tizoc. *Anales del Museo Na-*

cional de México, vol. I, pp. 3–38. Imprenta de I. Escalante, Mexico.

1877b Dedicación del Templo Mayor de México. *Anales del Museo Nacional de México*, vol. I, pp. 60–90. Imprenta de I. Escalante, Mexico.

PALACIOS, ENRIQUE JUAN

1929 La Piedra del Escudo Nacional de México. *Publicaciones de la Secretaría de Educación Pública*, tomo XXII, no. 9. Dirección de Arqueología, Mexico.

PANOFSKY, ERWIN

1960 Renaissance and Renascences in Western Art. Almquist and Wiksell, Stockholm.

POMAR, JUAN BAUTISTA DE

1964 Relación de Juan Bautista de Pomar (Tezcoco, 1582). *In* Poesía Náhuatl: Romances de los Señores de la Nueva España, Manuscrito de Juan Bautista de Pomar, Tezcoco, 1582 (Ángel Ma. Garibay K., ed.), vol. I, pp. 149–239. Instituto de Historia: Seminario de Cultura Náhuatl, Universidad Nacional Autónoma de México, Mexico.

RAMIREZ, JOSÉ FERNANDO (ed.)

1844–46 Appendix: Notas y esclarecimientos a la historia de la conquista de México del Señor W. Prescott. *In* Historia de la conquista de México, con una ojeada preliminar sobre la antigua civilización de los Mexicanos, y con la vida de su conquistador Fernando Cortés (W. Prescott). (Trans. by Joaquin Navarro.) Impreso por I. Cumplido, Mexico.

1885 Codex Chimalpopocatl; Anales de Cuauhtitlan; Noticias históricas de México y sus Conturnos. (Trans. by Faustino Galicia Chimalpopoca, Gumesindo Mendozo and Felipe Sánchez Solís.) Supplement to the *Anales del Museo Nacional de México*. Imprenta de I. Escalante, Mexico.

READ, CHARLES H.

1895 On an Ancient Mexican Head-piece, Coated with Mosaic. *Archaeologia*, vol. 54, pp. 383–398. London.

ROSENFIELD, JOHN, and SHUJIRO SHIMADA

1970 Traditions of Japanese Art: Selections from the Kimiko and John Powers Collection. Fogg Art Museum, Harvard University, Cambridge.

ROWE, JOHN HOWLAND

1962 Chavín Art: An Inquiry into Its Form and Meaning. The Museum of Primitive Art, New York.

SAHAGÚN, FRAY BERNARDINO DE

1951–70 Florentine Codex: General History of the Things of New Spain. (Trans. by Arthur J. O. Anderson and Charles E. Dibble.) 13 parts. *Monographs of The School of American Research*, No. 14. The School of American Research and the University of Utah, Santa Fe.

SAVILLE, MARSHALL H.

1922 Turquois Mosaic Art in Ancient Mexico. *Contributions from the Museum of the American Indian, Heye Foundation*, vol. VI. New York.

SELER, EDUARD

1902–23 Gesammelte Abhandlungen zur Amerikanischen Sprach- und Alterthumskunde. 5 vols. A. Asher and Co. and Behrend and Co., Berlin. (Reprint 1960–61: Akademische Druck- und Verlagsanstalt, Graz.)

SIMÉON, RÉMI

1885 Dictionnaire de la langue Nahuatl ou Mexicaine, rédigé d'après les documents imprimés et manuscrits les plus authentiques et précédé d'une introduction. Imprimerie Nationale, Paris. (Reprint 1963: Preface par Jacqueline de Durand-Forest, Akademische Druck- u. Verlagsanstalt, Graz.)

STIRLING, MATTHEW W.

1943 Stone Monuments of Southern Mexico. *Smithsonian Institution, Bureau of American Ethnology, Bulletin 138*. U.S. Government Printing Office, Washington.

VILLA ROJAS, ALFONSO

1968 Apéndice: Los Conceptos de Espacio y Tiempo entre los Grupos Mayances Contemporáneos. *In* Tiempo y Realidad en el Pensamiento Maya: Ensayo de Acercamiento (Miguel León-Portilla), pp. 119–167. Instituto de Investigaciones Históricas, Universidad Nacional Autónoma de México, Mexico.

VOGT, EVON Z.

1969 Zinacantan: A Maya Community in the Highlands of Chiapas. The Belknap Press of Harvard University Press, Cambridge.

WILLEY, GORDON R.

1973 Mesoamerican Art and Iconography and the Integrity of the Mesoamerican Ideological System. *In* The Iconography of Middle American Sculpture, pp. 153–162. The Metropolitan Museum of Art, New York.